Work-Based Learning

Level 2

/Q/SVQ
IPLOMA

PERFORMING ENGINEERING OPERATIONS   Mandatory Units

Mike Tooley

Richard Tooley

York College

000177052

ALWAYS LEARNING

PEARSON

Published by Pearson Education Limited, a company incorporated in England and Wales, having its registered office at Edinburgh Gate, Harlow, Essex, CM20 2JE. Registered company number: 872828

www.pearsonschoolsandfecolleges.co.uk

Text © Mike Tooley, Richard Tooley 2012
Typeset by Tek-Art, Crawley Down, West Sussex
Original illustrations © Pearson Education Ltd 2012
Illustrated by Tek-Art
The rights of Mike Tooley and Richard Tooley to be identified as authors of this work have been asserted by them in accordance with the Copyright, Designs and Patents Act 1988.

First published 2012

15 14 13 12
10 9 8 7 6 5 4 3 2 1

British Library Cataloguing in Publication Data

A catalogue record for this book is available from the British Library

ISBN 978 0 435 07506 4

Copyright notice

All rights reserved. No part of this publication may be reproduced in any form or by any means (including photocopying or storing it in any medium by electronic means and whether or not transiently or incidentally to some other use of this publication) without the written permission of the copyright owner, except in accordance with the provisions of the Copyright, Designs and Patents Act 1988 or under the terms of a licence issued by the Copyright Licensing Agency, Saffron House, 6–10 Kirby Street, London EC1N 8TS (www.cla.co.uk). Applications for the copyright owner's written permission should be addressed to the publisher.

Printed and bound in Spain by Grafos

Acknowledgements
Pearson Education Ltd would like to thank Simon Smith and the team at SOS Consultancy for their invaluable help in reviewing the technical content of this resource and the staff and students of Chichester College and Oaklands College for their patience and assistance in setting up the photo shoots for this book.

The publisher would like to thank the following for their kind permission to reproduce their photographs:

(Key: b-bottom; c-centre; l-left; r-right; t-top)

Alamy Images: Adrian Brockwell 69b, Conrad Elias 32, David J. Green 8, Gari Wyn Williams 61, Hemis 27c, Imagebroker 19, incamerastock 27t, 49, MBI 43, Nic Hamilton 22, Powered by Light / Alan Spencer 58; **Construction Photography:** Paul McMullin 65, 103; **Deb Limited:** 14tc; **Digital Vision:** 26b; **Getty Images:** Bloomberg 26t, PhotoDisk 13c; **Masterfile UK Ltd:** 25b, 59; **Pearson Education Ltd:** Clark Wiseman / Studio 8 13br, 14bl, 14br, 15tr, 15cl, 15cr, 15br, 18tl, David Sanderson 13cr, 14tl, 29tl, 29tr, 34, 35tr, Gareth Boden 21, 39, 40c, 40b, 82, Jules Selmes 10, 18cl, 38, 46, 48, 53, 54, 54tl, 57, 85, Naki Photography 6r, 36, 56; **Press Association Images:** AP / Kimimasa Mayama 71; **Science Photo Library Ltd:** Dr. P Marazzi 13tr; **Shutterstock.com:** Baloncici 41, Daniel Padavana 77, Dario Sabljak 69t, Elnur 18bl, Frances A. Miller 25t, Harald Høiland Tjøstheim 20l, Harald Hølland Tjøstheim 31, jennyt 35cr, Khukov Oleg 73, Kurhan 20r, Kuzma 1, Michael Shake 14cl, prism68 15c, ZENCKOphotography 75, Zhukov Oleg 45; **www.imagesource.com:** 6l

Cover images: *Front:* **iStockphoto:** Michael Fernhal

All other images © Pearson Education

Every effort has been made to trace the copyright holders and we apologise in advance for any unintentional omissions. We would be pleased to insert the appropriate acknowledgement in any subsequent edition of this publication.

Pearson would like to thank Jules Selmes and Adam Giles from Jules Selmes Photographer for their hard work and dedication throughout the photo shoots for this book.

Every effort has been made to contact copyright holders of material reproduced in this book. Any omissions will be rectified in subsequent printings if notice is given to the publishers.

Crown copyright material is reproduced with the permission of the controller of HMSO – pages 8, 28, 33

Contents

YORK COLLEGE

STAMPED X   CAT. JJ

ACC. No. 000177052

CLASS No. 620 TOU

EARNING RESOURCES 9/19
CENTRE

Introduction

Welcome to the exciting and challenging world of engineering!

The world that we live in and the machines and systems that we depend on were all designed, built and maintained by engineers. The cars, ships, trains and aircraft that we travel in and the phones that we rely on are all examples of the work of engineers. Think what life would be like without these things!

Engineers drive key technological change. They are in the front line in moving the UK, and other European countries, from a society dependent on high carbon, low security energy to a mix of wind, wave, nuclear, solar and carbon capture energy sources. We urgently need this change to be made, making engineers all the more important in the modern world.

Engineers are working to improve our transport infrastructure, including projects on high-speed rail travel, the development of low carbon vehicles, a national charging infrastructure for electric cars and other technologies that will revolutionise the way we live.

Engineering is a thriving sector of UK industry. It offers a very wide range of employment opportunities and is one area where there is no shortage of jobs. As an aspiring engineer you should be constantly questioning how and why things work the way they do and how they could be improved. We hope that this book will become a key part in this process.

About Performing Engineering Operations

Performing Engineering Operations (PEO) is an ideal first qualification in engineering that supports the delivery and assessment of the basic skills and knowledge required by a range of industries. PEO is available with qualifications at levels 1 and 2 and leads to a variety of pathways in line with the specific requirements of industrial sectors. This includes aerospace, transportation, and general manufacturing.

PEO is part of a long-established and highly respected framework of National Vocational Qualifications (NVQ). Many young people enter employment each year having followed the NVQ route and employers recognise the value of these qualifications in providing them with a competent and effective workforce.

About this book

This book has been produced to help you build a sound knowledge and understanding of all aspects of the NVQ in Performing Engineering Operations. The topics in this book cover all the information you will need to attain the three core Level 2 Units together with eight of the most popular optional units. Each chapter of the book relates to a particular unit and provides the information needed to form the required knowledge and understanding of that area. It can be used for any awarding organisation's qualification including BTEC and City & Guilds.

The book has been written by a team of experienced authors and trainers who have many years of experience within the engineering sector. They aim to provide you with all the necessary information you need to support your studies and to ensure that the information is presented in a way that makes it both relevant and accessible. Our aim has also been to make the book a useful reference tool for you in your professional life once you have gained your qualifications and are working in the engineering sector.

About the UK engineering industry

More than five million people work in the engineering sector in the UK, in a wide range of areas from transport to energy and even the space industry. There is currently a massive shortfall of engineers with the skills needed to take the country forward. These predicted shortages are most pronounced in energy, utilities and civil engineering. In the UK alone, more than 13 000 mechanical, automotive and aerospace engineers need to be recruited every year for our engineering industries to simply stand still and many more are needed in order to grow the UK economy. By 2017, over 580 000 new workers will be needed for the manufacturing sector alone.

It has also become apparent that we need engineers now more than ever in order to deal with the urgent problems of climate change, a growing population and dwindling supplies of fossil fuels. Future trends in engineering will be influenced by government commitments to combat the effects of climate change and at the same time meet our demand for energy. To meet this challenge, engineers will need to develop and exploit a range of new technologies.

Apprenticeships

Apprenticeships are a great way of learning and gaining experience. You can become an apprentice by being employed and working for a company that is active in any of the engineering sectors such as mechanical engineering, production engineering and electrical engineering.

Apprenticeships allow you to work and earn money while at the same time gaining a valuable nationally recognised qualification. You can begin an apprenticeship once you are 16 and it must be completed by your 25th birthday. Taking an engineering apprenticeship can open up a huge variety of different careers.

Depending on what job you decide to do, or which company you work for, an apprenticeship will involve you working and learning 'on the job' while at the same time attending a local college on a regular basis. An apprenticeship will give you a unique opportunity to demonstrate your ability to an employer and for them to get to know you while you are training. This has the advantage that many employers will want to offer you a permanent, full-time position when you've completed your apprenticeship qualification.

In addition to learning the skills relevant to your job, an apprenticeship will also allow you to build up new skills that will help you to develop your career. Being able to work with other people, and take responsibility for your own professional development, is just one part of this.

An important aspect of an apprenticeship is that, for much of the time, you will be working alongside experienced engineers and technicians who will show you how they do their jobs. The qualification that you will be studying will recognise your achievement and will help to show other people that you have the knowledge, competence and proficiency to work as an engineer.

About the authors

Mike Tooley is a technical author and consultant. He was formerly Dean of the Faculty of Engineering and Vice Principle at Brooklands College in Surrey, where he was responsible for the delivery of learning to over 9000 further and higher education students. Originally trained as an electronic engineer, Mike is now the well-known author of several popular engineering and related text books, including widely adopted course texts for BTEC, A-Level, GCSE, Diploma and NVQ qualifications in Engineering.

Richard Tooley is a lecturer, Course leader and ILT Champion at Chichester College. He has taught engineering at all levels from Entry to Degree across a range of disciplines. Previous publications include resources to support BTEC Level 2 and 3 qualifications as well as articles in national engineering magazines. A keen innovator, his passion for engineering and education drives him to aim to create work that can truly inspire and enthuse today's young engineers.

Qualification mapping grid

This table maps the content of this book to some of the most popular exam boards.

Chapter	EAL	Edexcel	City & Guilds
1. Working safely in an engineering environment	QPEO2/001	L/600/5781	301
			D/103/8765
2. Working efficiently and effectively in engineering	QPEO2/002	D/600/5784	302
			H/103/8766
3. Using and communicating technical information	QPEO2/003	M/600/5790	303
			K/103/8767

Features of this book

This book has been fully illustrated with artworks and photographs. These will help to give you more information about a concept or a procedure as well as helping you to identify a particular tool or material.

This book also contains a number of different features to help your learning and development.

Safety tips

These three features give you guidance for working safely with tools and equipment and in the workplace.

Keep it safe

Red safety tips indicate a PROHIBITION (something you **must not** do).

Keep It Safe

Blue safety tips indicate a MANDATORY instruction (something that you **must** do).

Keep It Safe

Yellow safety tips indicate a WARNING (hazard or danger).

Other features

Key terms

These are new or difficult words. They are picked out in **bold** in the text and then defined in the margin.

Did You Know

This feature gives you interesting facts about the engineering sector.

Quick Tip

These provide small suggestions and pieces of advice for practical work, suggesting possible tips for best practice.

Case Study

This feature provides examples of real-life working practice for you to read about and discuss.

Hands On

These provide short activities or tasks to test your understanding of the subject.

QUICK CHECK

These are questions that appear throughout the chapter, relating to the recent content of that chapter to see how you are getting along.

INDUSTRY FOCUS

This feature gives a detailed example of a person's experiences in the industry, or a company closely related to the content of the chapter, and allows you to see how you could use some of the knowledge you have gained to help you find your perfect career!

CHECK YOUR KNOWLEDGE

This is a series of multiple choice questions at the end of each chapter, in the style of the end of unit tests used by some exam boards.

1 Working safely in an engineering environment

Being an engineer is a great job and offers the chance to get involved in all sorts of exciting activities. However, you always have to remember that these activities can also be dangerous, involve using potentially harmful equipment and often mean working in an inhospitable environment. It is very important that an engineer always takes adequate care to work safely, with thorough planning, carrying out the task correctly and clearing up afterwards. An engineer must also know what to do in an emergency. A good engineer plans thoroughly, completes the work safely and lives to tell the tale!

In this chapter you will explore the essential working practices that will keep you and those around you safe. You will explore the many legal requirements and legislation surrounding health and safety as well as your roles and responsibilities as an engineer.

In this chapter you will learn about:

- what health and safety is
- legislation and regulations
- personal protective equipment (PPE)
- working safely
- manual handling

- warning signs
- hazards
- risk assessment
- fire
- first aid requirements

What is health and safety?

The basic idea of health and safety is that everyone should to be able to carry out their job without being worried about their safety. It covers a huge range of topics from basic human comfort to protection against potentially lethal machinery and substances. We know that engineering often involves more potentially hazardous activities than some other jobs. Therefore, for us as engineers, it is even more important to understand and adhere to health and safety requirements – as the result of something going wrong in our working environment could be very much worse than in our everyday lives.

You sometimes hear people complaining about health and safety – that it is 'over the top' or stops them doing a particular activity. However, the focus of health and safety is not to stop people from carrying out potentially harmful activities but to ensure that activities are carried out with appropriate management and controls in place so as to reduce the risk of something going wrong.

Health and Safety Executive (HSE)

The Health and Safety Executive (HSE) is a government agency that regulates and enforces health and safety legislation in the workplace. It is responsible for making sure that companies keep to the guidelines as well as researching health and safety and also updating and designing new legislation.

The HSE employs a number of inspectors whose job it is to visit companies to ensure that they are working safely and offer them advice. The inspectors are entitled to walk into an organisation at any time – without notice – and they have the power to investigate any part of a business. Employers and employees are duty bound to assist the inspector with their work. An inspector can take immediate action if they are not happy with their findings. If they find some minor issues they might simply discuss these with the employer and schedule to revisit at a later date to see improvement.

In the case of a more serious problem, the inspector can issue an improvement notice. An improvement notice states where a company has broken health and safety law and describes what must be done to remedy the situation. If a serious breach has been made, or the inspector has serious concerns for safety, they can issue a prohibition notice. This might prevent a particular machine, activity or section of a company operating or could even halt a whole business! An employer must then take urgent action to remedy the situation before the notice can be removed.

If an accident occurs, or an allegation of unsafe practice is made, one or more inspectors may be sent in to investigate and might begin legal proceedings against an employer if necessary. If a company is to be prosecuted the inspector would be called by the court to provide evidence in the form of their findings as to whether the company was operating lawfully in terms of health and safety.

Did you know?

A phrase that often appears in legislation is 'so far as is reasonably practicable.' This means that health and safety must be followed at all times, but must take a common sense, practical approach.

Hands On

Using the Internet, find out more about the HSE. What powers does it have of prosecution? What can those found guilty be punished with?

Legislation and regulations

Within the area of health and safety there are massive amounts of legislation and regulations that must be considered and followed at all times. Health and safety is a legal requirement and must be taken seriously by all companies, whether large or small. Failure to comply with health and safety legislation could lead to serious injury or death and companies can be fined millions of pounds, with the individuals responsible sent to prison if they are found to have been negligent. Some of the main items of health and safety legislation that you will study in this unit are outlined below and each will be highlighted where relevant as you read through the various aspects of health and safety in this chapter.

Legislation	Brief description	Page ref.
The Health and Safety at Work Act (HASAWA), 1974	This is the main health and safety legislation in the UK and acts like an umbrella to cover all of the subsequent regulations.	4
The Management of Health and Safety at Work Regulations, 1999	This details some of the employer responsibilities in terms of health and safety including carrying out risk assessments to identify hazards and help prevent accidents.	8
Workplace Health and Safety and Welfare Regulations, 1992	This covers the basic health and safety requirements of the working environment, e.g. temperature, space, light, safety and welfare.	6
Personal Protective Equipment (PPE) at Work Regulations, 2002	This describes the responsibilities of employers to provide and maintain appropriate PPE for the activities it carries out.	13
Manual Handling Operations Regulations (MHO), 1992	This covers the precautions and responsibilities of employers and employees when required to move heavy loads unassisted.	20
Provision and Use of Work Equipment Regulations (PUWER), 1998	This outlines the provision, maintenance, training and safety features of any equipment being used.	8
Display Screen Equipment Regulations (DSE), 1992	This covers the safe use of visual display units (VDUs) such as computer/laptop screens as well as those on portable equipment and machinery.	7
Reporting of Injuries, Diseases and Dangerous Occurrences Regulations (RIDDOR), 1995	Describes how major accidents, diseases and dangerous occurrences must be reported to the Health and Safety Executive (HSE).	11
Control of Substances Hazardous to Health (COSHH), 2002	This relates to the safe handling, storage and disposal of potentially dangerous substances.	9

Table 1.01 Main health and safety laws

There are many other regulations that relate to specific areas of engineering. Depending on the area of engineering in which you work, you have to keep up to date with the relevant legislation that covers the activities you are involved in.

These include:

- Electricity at Work Regulations (EAWR), 1989
- Control of Noise at Work Regulations, 1995
- Confined Spaces Regulations (CSR), 1997
- Lifting Operations and Lifting Equipment Regulations (LOLER), 1998
- Supply of Machinery (Safety) Regulations, 2005
- Work at Height Regulations, 2005

The relevant legislation and regulations will be highlighted in the individual specialist units that you study during your PEO course. Additionally, companies often formulate their own policies and procedures that support and expand on the overarching legislation. As an employee it is your responsibility to understand and follow them at all times.

Health and Safety at Work Act (HASAWA), 1974

The Health and Safety at Work Act is a UK Act of Parliament that was passed in 1974. It outlines the roles and responsibilities of employers and employees in terms of health and safety. It is a huge document (over 120 pages!) and it covers all of the main areas of health and safety. It is law and failure to comply with it is a criminal offence.

The Health and Safety at Work Act is an 'umbrella' act covering a number of other regulations.

Figure 1.01 Regulations that are covered by the Health and Safety at Work Act

Health and safety is the responsibility of us all – so it is important to know what you need to do to keep things safe! Table 1.02 summarises some of the main responsibilities of employers and employees from HASAWA, that relate to working in engineering.

Section 2: Employers	Section 7: Employees
All employers have a duty:	As an employee you have a duty:
• of care for the welfare, health and safety of their employees where it is practicable for them to do so	• to look after your own safety and that of your colleagues and people around them
• to provide and maintain safe equipment, tools and plant within the workplace	• not to intentionally or recklessly interfere with or misuse anything provided for your health and safety
• to ensure working conditions are safe and hygienic	• to take reasonable care at work for the health and safety of yourself and others who may be affected by what you do or do not do • to bring to your employer's attention any situation you consider dangerous
• to provide proper **personal protective equipment** (PPE) and make sure it is used correctly	• to use any PPE provided correctly
• to make sure articles and substances are used, handled, stored and transported safely	• to help the employer to meet their **statutory** obligations
• to provide any necessary information, instruction, training and supervision to ensure the health and safety of employees	• to co-operate with your employer on health and safety matters
• to make sure everyone can get in and out of the workplace safely	• to bring to your employer's attention any weakness in their welfare, health and safety arrangements
• to provide adequate facilities and arrangements for welfare at work	

Table 1.02 Summary of the duties of employers and employees

The employer must also:

- draw up a health and safety policy statement if there are five or more employees
- carry out risk assessments for all the company's work activities and review these (and record the assessments if there are five or more employees)
- identify and implement control measures, and tell employees about them
- consult with any official trade union safety representative
- establish a safety committee if requested by safety representatives.

> **Key term**
>
> **Statutory** – something that is set down in law and must be complied with

Workplace Health and Safety and Welfare Regulations, 1992

The regulations relate to the general working environment and employee welfare. The requirements include:

- good upkeep and cleanliness of facilities
- the provision of toilets and drinking water
- adequate ventilation and heating (a minimum working temperate of 16°C for desk work and 13°C for manual work)
- appropriate lighting including emergency lighting
- the control of roads and walkways around a business/site.

Hands On

How well is your environment maintained where you work? What changes could you make to make it more comfortable and how might this affect your productivity?

Figure 1.02 Health and safety and welfare is important both in offices and when working elsewhere

Display Screen Equipment Regulations (DSE), 1992

Engineers often spend long periods of time in front of computers as part of their job role. The DSE regulations require employers to make sure that workers are able to use them safely. The positioning of the keyboard, mouse and screen, along with inappropriate furniture, can cause workers to have a poor posture and is associated with repetitive strain injuries (RSI). Employers are required to provide good quality individually adjustable furniture so that all employees can adopt a correct working posture. Good lighting that avoids screen glare and adequate training is also required. The DSE regulations recommend frequent short breaks during prolonged use. Additionally, employees who regularly use display screen equipment are entitled to have eye tests funded by their employer.

> **Hands On**
>
> Take a look at your desk at home or work and assess it against the DSE recommendations. Try to arrange the furniture/equipment to make it better.

Working at a computer

These guidelines will help you to feel comfortable and keep safe when working at a computer.

- Keep your workspace clear and ensure that you have enough space to work.
- The screen should be at the same level as your eyes so that you can easily read it straight ahead of you.
- Position the screen or adjust lighting to avoid screen glare and reflections and keep it clean.
- You should be able to read your screen easily and comfortably. Adjust brightness/ contrast and software settings to achieve this if necessary.
- Keep the space under your desk clear so that your legs can move freely. Avoid pressure on the backs of your knees; a foot rest can help with this.
- Your keyboard and mouse should be positioned within easy reach. Your wrists should be roughly horizontal when typing or using the mouse. Avoid gripping the mouse or pressing buttons/keys with excessive force.

Figure 1.03 Good working posture is important for long-term health

The DSE regulations cover all types of display screens; for example the screen on a Computer Numerically Controlled (CNC) machine, the display on a piece of electronic test equipment or a video monitor are all included.

> **Hands On**
>
> Get a friend to take a photo of you when you are working at a computer workstation. Print out the picture and evaluate how you are working using the notes above to help you. What could you do to improve things?

Figure 1.04 All equipment must be set up correctly and checked before use

Figure 1.05 The Management of Health and Safety at Work Regulations, 1999

Provision and Use of Work Equipment Regulations (PUWER), 1998

The Provision and Use of Work Equipment Regulations (PUWER) describe how any equipment used in a workplace must be correctly provisioned, used and maintained. This applies to all equipment, from hammers to computer mice to industrial machinery. PUWER details that all equipment should:

- be fit for purpose, i.e. of good quality and 'the right tool for the job'
- be properly maintained and periodically inspected
- have clear safety signage and labelling
- have any dangerous parts appropriately guarded
- be able to be isolated from the electrical power supply (if applicable).

As an individual you should always carry out basic safety checks before you use any piece of equipment as well as ensuring it is still in good order when returned. When using machinery make sure that all guards are securely in place. Always make sure that you are familiar with any equipment that you need to use and, if necessary, seek advice and guidance from a senior colleague before setting out.

Management of Health and Safety at Work Regulations, 1999

These regulations further the HASAWA and underpin the requirements of companies to have comprehensive health and safety procedures in place. They describe how employers must have full and well-prepared risk assessments (see page 29) for all of the activities that they carry out, including provision for young people and expectant mothers. Emergency procedures and health and safety policies must be well designed, properly documented and taught to all staff who must in turn follow them. It also includes amendments that cover construction, mining and offshore industries.

Control of Substances Hazardous to Health (COSHH), 2002

Many substances that we use in engineering could cause us harm. These dangerous substances can enter our bodies in various ways:

- accidental ingestion (eating)
- breathing in gases, fumes, or airborne particles
- absorption through the skin or via cuts/grazes
- accidental injection
- eye contact.

Case Study

Bright Spark Electronics Ltd has assembled consumer electronic products for many years. The owners decide to develop a new area of their business and start manufacturing the circuit boards themselves rather than buying them in. The process of manufacturing the boards uses a chemical called ferric chloride and they have to decide on how to store, use and dispose of this chemical correctly to meet COSHH regulations. Below is an outline of their procedures.

Storage: The ferric chloride is supplied in a dry granular form, bulk packaged in vacuum sealed plastic bags. The contents are transferred into large screw-topped plastic jars so that they can be poured more easily when required and re-sealed safely – rather than leaving the remainder in the open plastic bag. The jars are clearly labelled with the contents and bear the appropriate chemical hazard labels. The jars are stored in a locked yellow metal cabinet that is also labelled with the hazard symbols for the contents. Materials data sheets are stored on a shelf next to the cabinet for easy access in an emergency.

Usage: Any workers using ferric chloride are given extra training. PPE requirements of latex gloves, safety goggles and plastic apron are expected and mandatory signage is put up in the work area to reflect this. The ferric chloride must be diluted in a solution before being poured into a special etching tank. The company provides weighing scales and measuring cylinders to ensure that the correct and safe solution strengths are made up. An overhead extraction system is installed and runs continuously. First aid and an eye wash station are nearby.

Disposal: Periodically the ferric chloride solution needs to be replaced. The solution is siphoned from the tank into large screw-top bottles that are clearly marked with the contents and appropriate hazard labels. The bottles are stored in the secured cabinet. A specialist disposal company visits the company every two weeks to collect the bottles for disposal.

Harm to our bodies might be immediate or develop years later as a result of prolonged use of a substance. Therefore we always need to take adequate care when working with any potentially harmful substances – even if we see no immediate threat. Appropriate PPE should be worn and local exhaust ventilation (LEV) may be required to remove gases/fumes/dust. LEV equipment must be maintained properly and tested at least annually.

Figure 1.06 A typical fume cupboard used to extract potentially harmful fumes and gases

Hazardous substances must be stored securely and be labelled clearly, including appropriate safety signage. CHIP (Chemicals Hazard Information and Packaging for Supply) regulations outline these responsibilities. The European standard for labelling hazardous substances consists of an orange box with a black pictogram. New CLP (Classification, Labelling and Packaging) regulation introduces a new international standard and this is currently in the process of phasing out the European standard. Therefore, you should be able to recognise either symbol and understand its meaning. Figure 1.07 shows both standards.

All hazardous materials should be supplied with a safety data sheet that details the nature of the hazard, precautions required and action to take in the event of accidental contamination or spillage. This should form part of the risk assessment for the activity for which the substance is required.

Figure 1.07 (a) European and (b) International Hazardous Substance labels

QUICK CHECK

1 **(a)** What is the minimum working temperature for working at a desk and for woodwork?
   (b) What regulations state this?
2 According to PUWER, what safety precautions must an employer take for a soldering iron?
3 Name three hazardous substances that you have used and for each give the relevant hazard symbol.

RMT CHEMICALS

Safety Data Sheet
Universal Solvent

Product Description

Product:	Universal Solvent
Product Code:	UVS01
Manufacturer:	RMT Chemicals, Unit A, Petworth Business Park, PC12 1AB, 01798 123 456
Chemical(s):	Propylenether
Appearance:	Clear liquid
Odour:	Etherlike

Warnings

  Flammable (flamepoint 38°C, ignition 290°C)

Safety Precautions

Storage:	Store securely in a cool well ventilated area.
PPE:	Wear chemical resistant gloves and safety goggles. Use in a well ventilated area away from sources of ignition and foodstuffs. Do not smoke.
Disposal:	Incinerate or specialist disposal.

Accidental Release Measures

Spillage:	Collect immediately, do not allow to enter drainage. Remove ignition sources.
Fire:	Use water or alcohol resistant foam extinguisher.

First Aid

Skin contact:	Wash thoroughly with soap and water.
Eye contact:	Flush with water. Seek immediate medical assistance.
Ingestion:	Drink water, do not induce vomiting. Seek immediate medical attention.
Inhalation:	Seek fresh air immediately.

Figure 1.08 Substance safety sheet

Reporting of Injuries, Diseases and Dangerous Occurrences Regulations (RIDDOR), 1995

It is important that when something out of the ordinary happens it is carefully recorded. This helps us to see any potential trends developing as well as learning useful lessons from what has happened. Typically all accidents (however small) are recorded in an accident book. The accident book may be reviewed and/or collated by the organisation's appointed health and safety officer who may take necessary action within the company. As a minimum an accident report should contain:

- the date and time of the accident
- what happened
- details of who was injured and what the injuries were
- details of any witnesses
- the reporter's name and signature.

Hands On

Imagine that an accident has happened at work. Create an accident report as you would for an internal accident book.

The Reporting of Injuries, Diseases and Dangerous Occurrences Regulations (RIDDOR) 1995 also state that certain serious injuries and occurrences must be reported centrally to the HSE itself. These include serious accidents involving major injury, breakouts of dangerous infectious disease and some specific medical issues. Certain dangerous occurrences (or near misses) must also be reported. An appointed person must make these reports formally as soon as possible and at least within 10 days. This can now be done over the phone or via the Internet. Table 1.03 outlines some of the notifiable items under RIDDOR.

Major injuries	Notifiable diseases	Dangerous occurrences
• Fracture or dislocation of main body parts (other than fingers or toes) • Amputation • Eye damage including burns (chemical or hot metal) and any penetrating eye wound • Injury from electric shock causing unconsciousness • Any injury causing unconsciousness, requiring CPR or hospital admittance for more than 24 hours • Unconsciousness caused by hazardous substance inhalation, ingestion or absorption through the skin • Illness caused by biological hazards, toxins or infected material • Injuries from any cause (however minor) that required the casualty to be away from work or incapable of fulfilling their full duties for a period of **over three days**	• Some types of poisoning • Work-related skin conditions such as dermatitis, skin cancer, chrome ulcer, and oil folliculitis/acne • Lung conditions including occupational asthma, farmer's lung, pneumoconiosis, asbestosis and mesothelioma • Certain infections including leptospirosis, hepatitis, tuberculosis, anthrax, legionellosis and tetanus • Other medical conditions caused as a result of work including occupational cancer, certain musculoskeletal disorders, decompression illness and hand-arm vibration syndrome	• Collapse of lifting equipment • Explosion caused by damage to a pressurised vessel • Explosions or collapse that extend beyond the boundary of company • Accidents involving contact with overhead power lines • Failure of radioactive equipment, e.g. X-ray machines • Failure of breathing apparatus • Accidental release of biological agents • Accidents involving vehicles transporting hazardous materials • Incidents at a well or pipeline

Table 1.03 Notifiable items under RIDDOR

QUICK CHECK

1 Explain why it is important to keep a record of accidents both with a company and centrally by the HSE.
2 Name five instances of accidents that would need to be reported to the HSE under RIDDOR.

Personal Protective Equipment (PPE)

Humans are fragile creatures and it is important to protect ourselves when working in an engineering environment. Personal protective equipment (PPE) includes things that we wear and/or use to help reduce the risk of harm (either immediate or long term) to our personal well-being. The Personal Protective Equipment at Work Regulations (1992) dictate that employers must supply and maintain appropriate PPE for any activities carried out. The PPE required differs depending on the activity being carried out and would be clearly defined in the risk assessment (see page 29). Additionally, mandatory signage may also indicate the appropriate PPE required in a given area (see pages 22–23). Some common types of PPE are described below.

Hand protection

It is very important that an engineer takes good care of his or her hands; after all, these are two of their most important tools! Continual harsh treatment and exposure to even mild industrial chemicals can lead to **dermatitis**, a painful dry, red and itchy skin condition.

Rigger gloves – often manufactured from tough fabrics or leather – are used to protect hands from physical damage during manual activities. Rubber coatings also help with grip and/or give chemical and liquid resistance. **Gauntlets** additionally protect lower arms and are thicker to provide thermal resistance, for example when welding or brazing.

Latex or **plastic gloves** protect against dirt and chemicals while allowing the wearer to retain some feeling and dexterity. Plastic gloves are often disposable and available in a range of sizes, thicknesses and chemical resistance properties. Note that some people can be allergic to latex. Therefore, you should take care to select them appropriately – depending on your preference.

Some engineers do find gloves a hindrance, especially when undertaking precise hand work that requires a high degree of accuracy and sensitivity. Additionally, there are circumstances when gloves are not recommended as they could get caught in machinery. An alternative to wearing gloves where harmful chemicals do not immediately threaten bare hands is **barrier creams**. Applied before starting to work, the barrier cream creates a thin barrier on the surface of the hands to protect them during the work.

When an engineer has completed any task their hands should be cleaned thoroughly. Specialist soaps are often used which help to break down oil/grease, with many containing fine grains to aid scrubbing. A scrubbing brush may also be used to remove stubborn deposits as well as cleaning under the nails. Once clean and dry a hand lotion may be applied to rehydrate and moisturise hands. This may all sound excessive but it is crucial to look after such an important asset. Hand washing is also important to avoid accidental consumption of chemicals; for example when eating with unclean hands.

Figure 1.09 Dermatitis can be a painful skin condition

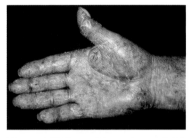

Figure 1.10 Rigger gloves

Figure 1.11 Gauntlet gloves

Figure 1.12 Latex gloves

SKIN SAFETY CENTRE

STEP 1
Protect
Apply to clean hands before work to help protect your skin and make easier to clean

STEP 2
Cleanse
Wash your hands regularly with the appropriate hand cleaner

STEP 3
Restore
Apply to clean hands after work to re-condition your skin

Figure 1.13 Hand care station

Now wash your hands please

Figure 1.14 Wash your hands sign

Similarly, you may hear lots of horror stories about engineers who did not wash their hands before visiting the toilet! In addition to this, good hand hygiene has been cited as an important factor in reducing the spread of illness and disease.

Eye protection

Eyes are very sensitive and are easily damaged by chemicals and penetrating objects as well as harmful radiation. **Safety spectacles/glasses** offer basic general protection from solid objects and minor splashes. However, **goggles** offer far better protection by sealing against the wearer's face. **Welding masks** shield the eyes and face from the extreme light and heat of welding as well as filtering out harmful UV radiation. Specialist filtered lenses may also be used when working with infrared and lasers.

Figure 1.15 Safety spectacles

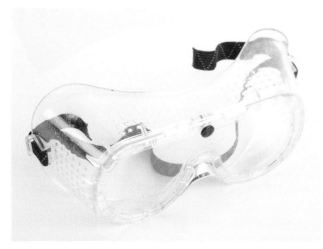

Figure 1.16 Safety goggles

Figure 1.17 Welding mask

Hearing protection

Our ears are incredibly sensitive organs and can be easily damaged. Sound levels of around 100 decibels (equivalent to the sound of a diesel truck or pneumatic drill) are enough to permanently damage hearing with minimal continued exposure. **Ear plugs** are usually disposable due to hygiene reasons and are commonly provided in a dispenser for general workshop use. **Ear defenders** offer greater noise reduction and can be more suited to outdoor work, where they also provide protection from the wind and cold. However, it is important to consider that using ear protection will also make it hard to hear more useful noises such as other workers, alarms or approaching vehicles. Therefore appropriate care must be taken.

Figure 1.18 Ear plugs

Respiratory protection

Our lungs are part of our critical life support system. Long-term inhalation of gases and particles can cause serious medical conditions such as asthma and cancer. The lungs can also stop working effectively very quickly if exposed to dangerous chemical gases, leading to unconsciousness and even death. **Extraction** and/or **air displacement systems** may be in place in a permanent workshop environment. Harmful gases may need to be filtered before being vented back to the environment. **Face masks** offer protection against airborne particles. Basic disposable masks offer cheap protection for large particulates such as wood dust. Higher grade filters, sometimes chemically active, are used in **respirators** used to protect against finer particles and some gases. They are commonly used when spray painting. If using extreme gases, or in confined areas, full **breathing apparatus** may be required.

Figure 1.19 Ear defenders

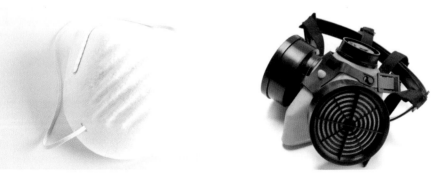

Figure 1.20 Disposable dust mask   Figure 1.21 Spray painting respirator

Head protection

Hard hats provide some protection from the impact of falling objects or if you hit your head against something sharp or hard. Hard hats can also contain in-built ear defenders and/or face shields. **Hair nets** may be used to keep longer hair from entanglement or to reduce dust contamination, for example in electronic component manufacture.

Figure 1.22 Hard hat

Figure 1.23 Safety boots

Figure 1.24 Lab coat

Figure 1.25 Hi-viz jacket

Hands On

Get someone to take a photo of you carrying out an engineering operation that requires the use of PPE. Create a poster using your photo to show the PPE used by labelling and justifying each PPE item.

QUICK CHECK

What PPE would you suggest for the following activities?

(a) Spray painting, (b) Electrical wiring on a building site, (c) Welding

Foot protection

Steel toe-capped shoes and boots protect feet from impact. It is important that you wear the correct size safety footwear for your feet in order to ensure comfort and to avoid painful rubbing that can occur due to the rigid toe plate. This is especially important if you are wearing them for many hours of hard work! For hygiene reasons you should avoid wearing anyone else's footwear. **Gaiters** and **spats** provide additional protection to the lower legs and are commonly used in heat-intensive activities such as forging.

Body protection

Protecting your body and clothing when you work is a basic continual PPE requirement. For machine and table-based activities **lab coats** may be adequate. However, more dirty and/or active pursuits such as working underneath a car or in a particularly dirty environment may necessitate full body protection, such as **overalls** or **boiler suits**. Heavy weight leather **aprons** may be worn for high temperature work. **Hazardous chemical (hazchem) suits** provide protection against airborne chemicals and particulates.

In many engineering activities, particularly when on site or outdoors it is important that an engineer can be seen by others. **High visibility** or **hi-viz garments** such as tabards (vests), jackets and suits may be worn. Typically these are brightly coloured yellow, green or orange with reflective strips. Garments may additionally offer thermal and waterproof protection to protect the wearer from the elements when working in inclement weather. During fine weather **sun cream** and **sunglasses** are also essential PPE to block damaging UV rays.

Provision and storage of PPE

It is the responsibility of the employer to provide their employees with appropriate and adequate PPE to support the activities that they must carry out. However, it is the individual responsibility of the employees to make sure that they actually wear it! It is essential that PPE is properly issued, stored and maintained to ensure that it remains up to standard. It should also be inspected before and after use. Using incorrect, unsuitable, broken or damaged equipment can offer reduced protection or even present its own risk to health. For example, scratched safety goggles could reduce visibility and ill-fitting garments/footwear might get entangled in equipment or cause a trip. Some large companies use vending machine style units to help easily store, issue and monitor PPE usage.

Working safely

As part of this unit, you will be assessed when working in an engineering environment to check that your safe working practices meet the right standards. In this book you can read all about the many different acts, legislation, regulations and standards involved in health and safety. These, along with any company policies, will need to be adhered to whatever your job role. However, this section offers some straightforward, down-to-earth advice for working safely in engineering. As you gain experience – in whatever area of engineering that you are involved in – you will also develop your own safe and professional way of conducting your work.

Knowing your environment

Whether you are working on an unknown building site or in your everyday place of work, you should make yourself fully familiar with your surroundings. Identify the emergency exits and the location of emergency equipment such as fire alarms, emergency stops, fire extinguishers and first aid equipment. Make sure that your evacuation route is clear and that you know what to do and who to contact in the case of an emergency.

Preparing to work

Benjamin Franklin, one of the founding fathers of the USA famously said: 'By failing to prepare, you are preparing to fail' – this is very true in engineering. Start by ensuring that you have the appropriate PPE for the job you are about to carry out. Your PPE should be in good condition and well fitting; overly tight clothing could limit your movement but baggy or loose clothing could get caught in machinery or cause you to trip. If you have long hair it should be tied back and any jewellery should be removed, tucked away or taped securely. Hands should be cleaned before starting work and barrier cream applied if not using gloves.

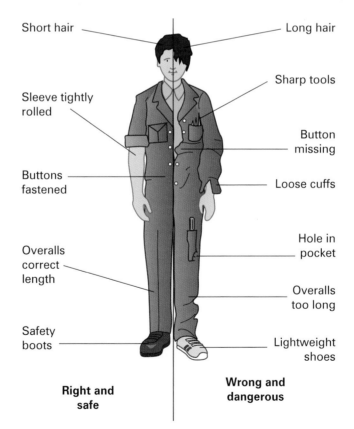

Short hair — Long hair

Sleeve tightly rolled

Sharp tools

Button missing

Buttons fastened

Loose cuffs

Overalls correct length

Hole in pocket

Overalls too long

Safety boots

Lightweight shoes

Right and safe

Wrong and dangerous

Figure 1.26 Good/bad PPE

Collect the required tools, equipment, materials and documentation before you begin. You do not always know who might have used the work area, tools, equipment or machinery before you. Therefore, you cannot guarantee that they have been left in a safe manner. For this reason you should always take time to check these carefully prior to starting work. Remember that the quality and condition of tools and equipment ultimately affects the quality of the finished work.

Acting responsibly

As an engineer you have a duty of care to act sensibly and considerately when you are working. Therefore the behaviours in the spidergram should be avoided in an engineering environment.

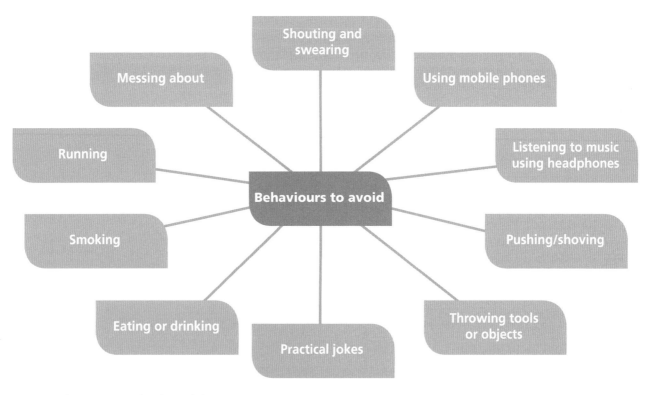

Figure 1.27 Behaviours to avoid in the workplace

Do the job properly

You must always follow the correct procedure for a job and work to the appropriate standards. It is important always to use the correct tool for the job, never 'make do' as this could damage the tool and/or compromise the quality or safety of your work. You should make use of supporting documentation and continually evaluate the quality of your work. Do not be tempted to cut corners or rush a job and never let safe working practices slacken in order to get something finished in a hurry – whatever the pressure you are under.

Hands On

Work with a partner and take turns to observe each other while you work. At the end of your session discuss how you feel each of you was working in terms of safe working practices. Try to come up with at least two ways that you could improve your professional practice.

Good housekeeping

Organisation is a key attribute of a good engineer. You should always make sure your workspace is clean and tidy, particularly keeping exits and gangways clear. Avoid cluttering your work area with too many tools and materials at any one time and clear up as you go. In particular, liquid spills such as oils or coolant should be dealt with immediately to remove a potential slip hazard. When you have finished work, clean and return your tools and clean down machinery – making sure that it is left in a safe condition. Any waste materials should be disposed of appropriately. Where appropriate, your work pieces should be clearly labelled/marked and stored accordingly.

Figure 1.28 Your work area should be clear and tidy at all times

QUICK CHECK

Write a bullet list of ten important points that an engineer should follow when working safely.

Know your limitations

Every engineer has different skills, abilities and experience. It is important to know where your limits are both physically and in terms of your skills. Another engineer or manager may assume that you know how to do something that you have no experience of. However, you must never attempt any activity that you are not confident that you can carry out safely and to a good standard. One of the golden rules in engineering is that if you are unsure about something, ask!
It is far better to ask for advice beforehand than to ask for an ambulance afterwards.

Manual handling

As an engineer, at some point you will inevitably need to move around heavy objects such as tools, equipment, materials or components. Manual handling includes lifting up, setting down, pushing, pulling, carrying and moving loads. Many workplace injuries relate in some way to inappropriate or poor manual handling. Lifting even relatively small weights incorrectly can cause serious damage. People are often tempted to lift heavier loads than they can do safely and this is often when injuries occur.

When possible you should avoid moving heavy loads unaided and use mechanical lifting aids to help you, such as pallet trucks, winches and sack barrows. Do, however, remember that although aids may help to move objects they do not entirely eliminate the effort or risk involved and appropriate care should still be taken. Particular care must be taken when working on uneven surfaces or slopes. Opposite is some practical advice for good lifting and carrying technique.

Hands On

Following the advice on page 21, practise your safe lifting and putting down technique using an empty cardboard box. Get a friend to video you and play it back to help you improve your technique.

Figure 1.29 Pallet truck   Figure 1.30 Sack barrow

1. Always check the nature of the object to be lifted before going straight in to lifting it; objects can be heavier than they appear. If you think that lifting aids and/or assistance might be required do not attempt to lift unaided.

2. Clear your path to where the object is to be moved to and make sure that you have adequate space to set it down. Adopt a secure stance with the legs shoulder-width apart either side of the object.

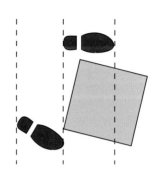

3. Keeping your back straight, bend your legs and get a solid grip on the object with arms straight out.

4. Begin to lift the object by extending the legs straight and keeping the back straight.

5. Move smoothly to your destination, keeping the object close to the body at waist height. Avoid jerky movements and never run.

6. When putting down, do so steadily, bending the legs rather than flexing the back (as with lifting). Remember that putting down can be as hazardous as lifting!

Hands On

Use your phone or camera to take as many photos of warning signs that you can find around your school/college workshop in five minutes. When your time is up, compare the number with the rest of your class. Now classify the different signs according to each type: hazard, mandatory, prohibition, fire, safe condition, hazardous substance.

Warning signs

In any engineering context good signage is essential. Signs warn us of potential hazards and indicate what precautions we should take. They help us to know what is safe to do and what is not in a particular area. They point out where we can get help and guide us to safety in an emergency. Signage helps employees to remember how to work safely and is essential to help visitors and new staff to learn about an unknown environment. Adequate signage is a key element in any organisation's health and safety policy and it is a simple and effective way to ensure compliance.

Safety Signs and Signals Regulations

We see signs everywhere we look and we probably know the meaning of several hundred of them without even thinking! However, what you probably never think about is what makes up a sign and what different types of signs there actually are. The Safety Signs and Signals Regulations define these. **Pictograms** are commonly used to visually represent what a sign is all about. In this way someone who cannot understand English could interpret the sign without actually having to read it. However, often the meaning is also written underneath for good measure. The colour and shape of a sign varies depending on the intended meaning. There is a set standard way to represent several different types of signs which is explored below.

Hands On

Design your own warning sign – it can be for any purpose but it must be drawn to the correct standards according to its meaning…but don't include any text, just a pictogram! Once your sign is ready, share it with the rest of the class and see if they can tell you what its meaning is.

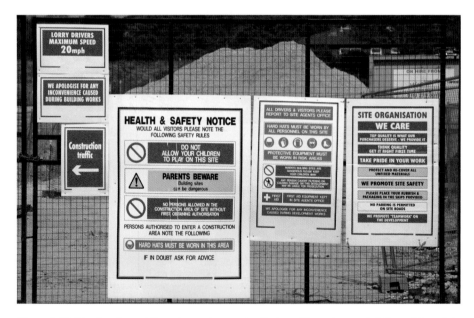

Figure 1.31 Warning signs at the entrance to a works site to notify workers and visitors of the safety precautions before entering

Key terms

Pictogram – when a picture is used to represent a meaning rather than text

Mandatory – something that must be done

Prohibited – something that must not be done

Hazard

Hazard signs (sometimes simply referred to as warning signs) are used to warn people of a potential hazard. They are triangular in shape with a black border and pictogram.

Mandatory

Mandatory signs are circular with a blue background and white pictogram and text (if included). They are used to tell people that they *must* do something, i.e. it is mandatory. For example 'wear ear defenders', 'guards must be in place', 'now wash hands' – all demand that an action is taken.

Prohibition

Prohibition signs are essentially the opposite of mandatory signs; they tell us what we *must not* do, i.e. something that is **prohibited**. Common examples include 'no smoking' and 'do not run'. They are characterised by a red outlined circle with a line through it containing a black pictogram.

Fire

Fire signs are solid red with white images and text. They are used exclusively to indicate fire-related devices and equipment such as fire alarm buttons, extinguishers, hoses etc. It is important to note that fire exit signs are not classified within this group; this is explained below.

Safe condition

Safe condition signs are used whenever there is a need to sign something relating to either making safe or getting to safety in the case of an emergency. For example, emergency stop buttons, fire exits, evacuation points and first aid equipment are all classified in this group. Safe condition signs are green with white images and text.

Hazardous substance signage

All substances that are hazardous to health must be correctly packaged, identified and labelled. There are currently two types of hazardous substance warning symbols. The European standard is an orange box with a black pictogram. However, these are currently being phased out in favour of the new international standard which has a red bordered diamond with black pictogram. You should be able to identify and understand both (see also COSHH page 10).

Hands On

Next time you are in the kitchen take a look in the cupboard under the sink and examine the back of some of the bottles/tins of cleaning products that you have. Note how they have been labelled to make users aware of the hazardous chemicals used inside. Which has the most warning signs?

Type of sign	Examples	
Mandatory	Hearing protection must be worn	Protective footwear must be worn in this area
Hazard		 RADIOACTIVE
Prohibition		
Fire	Fire alarm	
Safe condition	Fire assembly point	

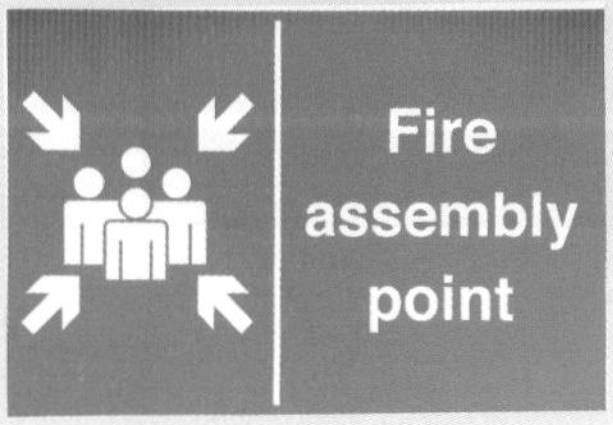

Figure 1.32 Safety signs

QUICK CHECK

1 Name three signs for each classification type: hazard, mandatory, prohibition, fire and safe condition.

2 Suggest appropriate signage for: **(a)** a bench drill, **(b)** a welding bay, **(c)** a building site.

Hazards

A hazard is anything that has the potential to cause harm to you or others when carrying out an activity. As part of this unit you will need to demonstrate your ability to identify and control hazards in your own working environment. Hazard identification is an essential part of risk assessment and this will be looked at in the next section (see page 29). Hazards vary greatly depending on what activities are being carried out and the environment in which they are carried out. Some general hazards in an engineering environment are described below.

Case Study

People are often confused by the difference between a hazard and a risk. In fact the terms are often used interchangeably although they are different. Essentially a hazard is anything that has the potential to cause someone harm whereas the risk is what the hazard could cause to happen. Below are some simple real-life examples to illustrate this principle.

Can you think of some more?

Scenario	Hazard	Risk
Office	Trailing electrical cables across a gangway	People could trip over cables, causing injury
Delivery driver	Driver works alone	No one to call for help in the event of driver incapacity No one to assist lifting heavy or bulky items that could cause injury if lifted improperly by an individual
Servicing a boiler	Flammable gas	Explosion Asphyxiation
Altering house wiring	Dangerous voltages	Electric shock

Hands On

List as many potential hazards as you can find around your place of study/work. For each hazard, note how you might be able to reduce or control the hazard.

Engineers are often required to work in environments that are potentially dangerous by their very nature. Two examples are working at height and confined spaces.

Working at height

Working at height includes any activity that is carried out from a position where a fall could cause injury. Falling from height is the single biggest cause of workplace deaths and a major cause of serious injuries. Therefore it is an area requiring additional consideration. The Working at Height Regulations introduced in 2005 outline that:

- working at height should be avoided if at all possible
- where it is not avoidable use appropriate equipment and take measures to prevent falls or minimise the distance of fall
- full risk assessments should be carried out
- any work at height must be properly planned, including emergency procedures
- safety equipment used is properly maintained, set up, inspected and used appropriately which might involve specialist staff training
- the weather conditions are taken into account
- care should be taken when working on fragile surfaces
- care should be taken to ensure nothing falls from the working area, e.g. tools, equipment, materials.

Figure 1.33 Harnesses are a good safety tool for working at height

Confined spaces

Confined spaces are not just 'small spaces' – they include any environment with closed or compromised boundaries, which place restrictions on access and egress. So caves, pressure vessels, tanks, silos, ventilation systems, industrial piping and sewers are all examples of confined spaces. Cramped, hot or humid conditions can also have implications for health, as well as making manual operations difficult. Hazards might include those from trapped gases already present or a build up of gases caused by the activity taking place, e.g. fumes from welding. For example, sewer workers wear a special gas detector to warn them of explosive gases, the lack of oxygen, and hydrogen sulphide gas that can cause asphyxiation. In fluid-based systems, water hazards also exist with a potential risk of drowning.

Figure 1.34 Confined spaces can restrict you when working

Figure 1.35 A mining air ventilation system

Figure 1.36 Care must be taken when carrying out work in high temperature conditions

Control measures for confined spaces might include specialised training, breathing equipment, gas detectors and restricting the time during which a worker should be in the confined space. Temporary ventilation or extraction systems may be installed to ensure a safe air supply to workers. This is often used in mining operations where large numbers of workers need to be able to work in the confined space and individual breathing apparatus would be unsuitable and costly. A 'permit to work' system may be used to keep track of who has entered a confined space, what they are to do and when they must return. If they do not return and 'clock out' immediate action can be taken to investigate.

Hot work

Many industrial processes and engineering environments involve operating within or around heat. Heat can have a dramatic effect on the human body. High temperatures can burn and ignite clothing on contact, with continued low exposure leading to dehydration and skin burns. Adequate care should be taken and workers should closely follow their company guidelines including wearing the appropriate PPE, following set procedures, keeping hydrated and knowing safe distances and exposure times.

QUICK CHECK

Describe the hazards when working in one of the following adverse environments:
- inspecting the inside of a pressure vessel
- welding a girder on a skyscraper
- hot metal working in a foundry.

Tools and equipment

The tools and equipment that engineers use can often present potential hazards. Even basic hand tools may be sharp, pointed or heavy. Therefore care should be taken when using, storing, and transporting them, as well as maintaining them correctly. Never carry tools in your pockets and never use damaged or blunted tools. Clean, maintain and inspect any equipment before and after use reporting any problems immediately. Returning damaged tools could cause serious harm to the next user if they fail to check them prior to use.

Powered tools and machinery may represent more severe hazards. Electrical hazards may be present with powered portable equipment as well as the power cables providing a trip hazard. Any portable electrical items must be periodically inspected and tested by a qualified electrical engineer to verify their electrical integrity. This is known as Portable Appliance Testing or PAT.

Cutting, grinding and sawing faces could cause grazing, cuts or amputation. Exposed moving parts could catch loose clothing, hair or jewellery causing harm and possibly pull workers into the machinery causing further severe injury. Swarf, chips and poorly held work can be ejected from machines and are also potential hazards. For this reason equipment must be clearly signed to indicate potential hazards in addition to having guards to protect workers both from gaining access into, and items ejecting from, a machine.

Figure 1.37 A PAT unit

Figure 1.38 Exposed belt drives on an antique combine harvester – this would never be allowed today!

(a) Guard fitted to a pillar drill

(b) Guard fitted to a cutter

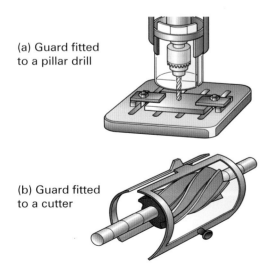

(c) Guard fitted to the drive belt of a power guillotine

(d) Guard fitted to the revolving bar of a lathe

Revolving bar

Barrier

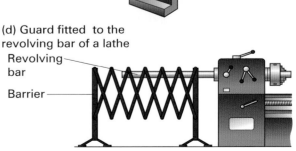

Figure 1.39 Various guarding techniques

Human error

Humans can make mistakes and knowingly or unknowingly do things incorrectly which could cause a hazard. The use of alcohol/drugs, stress and tiredness can affect our ability to work safely and make important decisions. Therefore it is important that we deal effectively with any of these issues should they become evident. Time pressure, laziness or ignorance might lead to 'cutting corners'. But failing to follow laid-down procedures in full can be very dangerous and should never be done. Guidelines and regulations have been designed for a reason and should be taken seriously and followed.

Hazardous materials/substances

As described in COSHH (page 9) engineers often use potentially dangerous materials and these obviously present specific hazards. Referencing the substance safety sheet and any appropriate company policy should inform workers of how to protect themselves and how to use and dispose of the material safely. Volatile and flammable substances could cause fire or explosion. Harmful, irritant, toxic and biologically hazardous substances may pose immediate or prolonged health risks. Sometimes seemingly 'safe' substances can cause harm, such as cutting fluids/oils which can cause adverse skin conditions.

Slip and trip hazards

Tripping and slipping over are very common causes of workplace injury. Keeping your work area clear and tidy as you go along will help to reduce the risk of someone tripping over objects. Avoid running cables or hoses along the floor, particularly across gangways and exit routes. Battery-operated equipment may be better in order to reduce cabling in an external environment and many dedicated workshops have overhead power/pneumatic supplies so that cables can simply be 'dropped down' where required. Keep emergency routes clear at all times. Take care on uneven or sloped surfaces. Wearing steel toe-capped boots with good-quality soles will aid grip. Spills of fluids, especially oil-based fluids, should be cleared up properly and immediately.

Any risk of tripping up could be a BIG problem in the workplace

TOP TIPS
→ CLEAN SPILLAGES IMMEDIATELY
→ KEEP WALKWAYS CLEAR
→ TIDY UP AS YOU GO
→ REPORT LEAKS, OBSTRUCTIONS AND DAMAGED FLOORS
→ DON'T LEAVE IT TO OTHERS

DON'T JUST SEE IT, SORT IT.
visit www.watchyourstep.hse.gov.uk or call 0845 345 0055

HSE
Better health & safety benefits everyone

Figure 1.40 HSE trip poster

Figure 1.41 Common slip and trip hazards

Hands On

Using the notes on the previous pages as a guide, create a mind map of the hazards associated with each of the activities/areas covered.

Fire

Fire hazards and fire-risk assessments are discussed on page 31.

Risk assessment

Whereas a hazard is something that has the potential to do harm, the risk is what the hazard could cause and how likely it is to happen. The idea of a risk assessment is to look at a particular activity to see what the potential hazards are, how likely they are to happen and what we can do to reduce them happening. It is a legal requirement and must be carried out for each activity undertaken.

A risk assessment generally involves the following five steps:

1. describe the activity including the working environment, tools, equipment and PPE required
2. identify the potential hazards
3. identify who the hazards might affect and how
4. decide on control measures to take to minimise risk
5. give the activity an overall risk factor (see below).

Control measures

A control measure is something put in place to try to reduce the risk of harm due to a hazard. Risk assessments should be recorded formally and kept where they can be easily accessed and are required to be reviewed periodically. Generally companies have their own risk assessment paperwork and well-defined procedures. You should always check the specific requirements with your employer before carrying out a risk assessment.

Risk factor

The risk factor is an indication of the overall safety of an activity based on both how likely an injury is to happen and how bad that injury would be. For example, an activity with the potential to kill somebody but extremely rarely might have the same factor as one that causes minor injuries but very frequently. Generally an activity will be graded as low, medium or high risk. If a risk assessment is undertaken and an activity is found to be medium or high risk, company policy may dictate that the activity must be approved by a health and safety officer before it can be carried out. There are various systems for helping you to grade the risk factor of an activity. Below is a simple but effective method where the likelihood and severity of injury are both scored from 1 to 3 and the overall risk factor is calculated by multiplying the two together. The resulting figure is then referenced to give low, medium or high risk.

Hands On

Carry out a risk assessment for a simple engineering activity that you are familiar with. Ask to see your training provider or employer's risk assessment for the same activity and see how they compare.

LIKELIHOOD	
1	Unlikely
2	Possible
3	Probable

Score: [ ]

SEVERITY	
1	Minor
2	Serious
3	Critical

Score: [ ]

RISK FACTOR	
1–3	Low risk
4–5	Medium risk
6–9	High risk

$$\times \quad \boxed{} \quad = \quad \boxed{}$$

Risk factor: [ ]

Figure 1.42 Risk factor matrix

QUICK CHECK

1 What is mean by the term risk factor?
2 Why might an activity that could only cause minor injuries have a high risk factor?
3 Why are risk assessments so important?

Risk Assessment

Details of assessor

Name:	Signature:	Date of assessment:
Gordon Jones	GFJones	3rd September 2012

Details of activity

Activity name:	Activity location:
Circuit board assembly line	Spark Electronics - Workshops A & B

Description of activity:
Assembly and hand soldering of consumer electronic products

Hazard identification

Hazards identified	Control measures in place to minimise
Fumes from solder flux could cause irritation and prolonged exposure is linked with occupation asthma. Aerosol flux cleaner is harmful if inhaled.	Permanent extraction system in place and inspected annually.
Electrical safety of portable equipment.	All equipment inspected before and after use. PAT testing carried out every six months. Broken or damaged equipment removed and logged.
Heat from soldering iron/solder could cause burns or start fire.	No flammable substances kept in vicinity. Soldering irons kept in stands when not in use. Equipment left to cool before storage. Lab coats worn to protect clothing and long hair tied back.
Trailing wires from equipment could cause trip hazard.	Dedicated bench-top power sockets used to minimise cable runs.
Sharp leads ejected during component trimming could cause eye damage if penetrating.	Safety spectacles worn by technicians.

Hazardous substances	Tools/equipment required	PPE required
Solder (containing flux) De-flux aerosol spray	Hand soldering equipment (soldering iron, side cutters, long-nosed pliers etc.)	Safety spectacles Lab coat Extraction system Anti-static wrist/leg strap

Risk factor assessment

Likelihood:	Severity:	Risk Factor (Likelihood x severity:
1 = unlikely to happen	1 = minor injury	1-3 = Low risk
2 = could possibly happen	2 = serious injury	4-5 = Medium risk
3 = likely to happen	3 = life critical injury	6-9 = High risk
Score:	Score:	Result:
2 - unlikely to happen	1 - minor injury	2 x 1 = 2 - low risk

Figure 1.43 Example risk assessment

Fire

Fire can spread quickly and easily get out of control. It is therefore very important to take action to avoid fire breaking out and know how to deal with it quickly and effectively if it does. There is also a need to know how to escape effectively in the event of fire.

Figure 1.44 In the event of a fire like this what would you do?

Figure 1.45 A fire detector being tested

Fire regulations

The 2005 Regulatory Reform (Fire Safety) Order (RRFSO) applies to all businesses, public places and shared housing. According to the Order the following are mandatory.

- Fire-risk assessments are carried out and reviewed periodically.
- Fire risks are identified and reduced or removed if possible.
- Flammable or explosive substances are stored securely and appropriately.
- Emergency evacuation plans are created, maintained and communicated to those who use the area.
- Fire drills should be used a method of testing and practising procedures.
- Records are kept and reviewed of any fire-related incidences.
- Emergency exits and routes are clearly marked and kept clear.
- Appropriate fire detection and fire safety equipment is installed and maintained.

Causes of fire

The 'fire triangle' is often used to illustrate the way in which a fire can begin. The three sides represent the three requirements that fire needs: oxygen, heat and fuel. Oxygen, readily available in the air, is required for a flame to burn whereas heat is required for the initial ignition of a flame. Fuel represents whatever flammable material is available to combust. We can therefore prevent fire from breaking out by ensuring that not all of the requirements are available at once. For example flammable materials (fuel) may be stored away from sources of ignition (heat).

Figure 1.46 A fire triangle

As part of a fire-risk assessment the locations of fuels and sources of ignition are identified as well as other fire risks and the location of staff that would be affected. This would help to make a plan of action to minimise risk and introduce further safety systems. The figures below show a small business before and after a fire-risk assessment and improvement plan has been carried out. In many cases relatively simple changes have made a real difference to fire safety.

Before a fire-risk assessment

After a fire-risk assessment

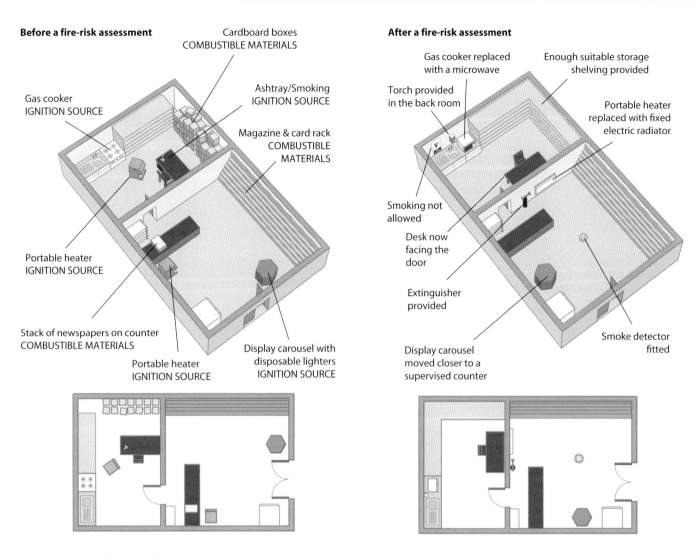

Cardboard boxes
COMBUSTIBLE MATERIALS

Ashtray/Smoking
IGNITION SOURCE

Gas cooker
IGNITION SOURCE

Magazine & card rack
COMBUSTIBLE
MATERIALS

Portable heater
IGNITION SOURCE

Stack of newspapers on counter
COMBUSTIBLE MATERIALS

Portable heater
IGNITION SOURCE

Display carousel with
disposable lighters
IGNITION SOURCE

Gas cooker replaced
with a microwave

Enough suitable storage
shelving provided

Torch provided
in the back room

Portable heater
replaced with fixed
electric radiator

Smoking not
allowed

Desk now
facing the
door

Extinguisher
provided

Display carousel
moved closer to a
supervised counter

Smoke detector
fitted

Figure 1.47 Before/after fire risk assessment

Firefighting equipment

The principle of fire extinguishers is simple. Returning to the fire triangle, if one of the three requirements for fire can be removed then it will extinguish. For example, carbon dioxide (CO_2) fire extinguishers work by removing the oxygen and water extinguishers work by removing the heat. Fire extinguishers are available in different types (identified by different colours) depending on the fire hazards in the intended area of use. Table 1.04 describes the main types.

Hands On

Have you ever actually used a fire extinguisher? If not, talk to your employer or local fire brigade about doing a course – you'll get to play with all of the different types of firefighting equipment that you can't normally fiddle with!

Standard/multi-purpose dry powder

Stripe colour	Blue
Application	Powder 'knocks down' the flames. Safe to use on most kinds of fire. Multi-purpose powders are more effective, especially on burning solids; standard powders work well only on burning liquids
Dangers	Powder does not cool the fire well. Fires that seem to be out can re-ignite. Doesn't penetrate small spaces, such as those inside burning equipment. Jet could spread burning fat or oil around
How to use	Aim jet at the base of the flames and briskly sweep it from side to side

Water

Stripe colour	Red
Application	Water cools the burning material. Only use water on solids, such as wood or paper. Never use water on electrical fires or burning fat or oil
Dangers	Water can conduct electricity back to you. Water actually makes fat or oil fires worse – they can explode as the water hits them
How to use	Aim the jet at the base of the flames and move it over the area of the fire

Carbon dioxide (CO_2)

Stripe colour	Black
Application	Displaces oxygen with CO_2 (a non-flammable gas). Good for electrical fires as it doesn't leave a residue
Dangers	Pressurised CO_2 is extremely cold. DO NOT TOUCH. Do not use in confined spaces
How to use	Aim the jet at the base of the flames and sweep it from side to side

Foam/AFFF (Aqueous Film Forming Foam)

Stripe colour	White or cream
Application	Foam forms a blanket or film on the surface of a burning liquid. Conventional foam works well only on some liquids, so not good for use at home. Very effective on most fires except electrical and chip-pan fires
Dangers	'Jet' foam can conduct electricity back to you though 'spray' foam is much less likely to do so. Foam could spread burning fat or oil around
How to use	For solids, aim jet at the base of the flames and move it over the area of the fire. For liquids, do not aim foam straight at the fire – aim it at a vertical surface or, if the fire is in a container, at the inside edge of the container

Table 1.04 Types of fire extinguisher

Notes on using fire extinguishers:

Using the wrong type of fire extinguisher on a fire can harm you and make the fire worse – only use one if you are confident in your selection and ability. You should never use a water extinguisher on a fat/oil fire as it will case the fire to flare dangerously. A fire blanket or damp cloth should be used to smother the fire instead. Fire blankets may also be used if a person is on fire. Water extinguishers should *never* be used on electrical fires as the water could conduct electricity back to the user and cause a shock.

Fire extinguishers must be checked periodically and 'topped-up' or replaced if required. A ring pull wrapped by a plastic tamper guard shows if a fire extinguisher has been tampered with. Never tamper or play with a fire extinguisher.

Figure 1.48 Fire blanket

Evacuation

If you discover a fire (other than the most minor) your priority should be in raising the alarm and informing others rather than trying to tackle it yourself. Alert more qualified staff and use a 'break glass' to trigger the alarm.

Figure 1.49 Break glass point

> ### Hands On
>
> Thinking about where you work, draw a map showing your evacuation route. Take time to walk through the route – checking for a clear path, correct signage and exits as you go. Are there any improvements that your could make?

All institutions have a set down evacuation plan that all employees should know. Green safety signage will direct you to the nearest fire exit and assembly point. Emergency lighting will activate in the event of power loss. If required to evacuate, do so calmly, orderly and with urgency but never run. Remain at your assembly point so that you can be accounted for (if you were to leave it might be assumed that you were still inside!). Never return to a building before the all-clear has been given. If you have information about the fire, for example its cause, location or anyone who may still be in the building, you should tell your supervisor or manager immediately so that it can be passed on to the attending fire brigade.

Figure 1.50 Evacuation route sign

QUICK CHECK

1 What are the legal requirements of a company in terms of fire?
2 List four different types of fire extinguisher and give uses for each.

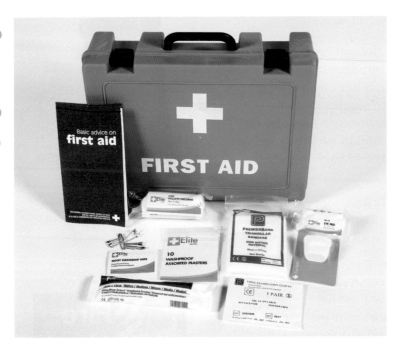

Figure 1.51 First aid box with contents

First aid requirements

Accidents can happen at any time when you are at work. The Health and Safety (First Aid) Regulations 1981 stipulate that any employer must provide adequate first aid equipment and personnel to be able to deal with an accident. As a minimum, employers must provide a properly stocked and maintained first aid box as well as having someone responsible for first aid arrangements and providing information and training to staff about first aid procedures.

It is important to note that this section will give you some brief guidance on first aid, but there is no substitute for having a first aid qualification.

The type and quantity of contents for a first aid box would depend on the number of people and type of environment or activities that it is designed to support. Products contained within a first aid box vary but typically might include:

Figure 1.52 First aid box sign

- plasters
- sterile dressings and bandages
- eye wash and pads
- medical tape and scissors
- face shield/mask
- disposable gloves
- maintenance record
- first aid leaflet.

First aid boxes should be inspected periodically and any depleted stocks replenished. Additionally, many items in a first aid box have an expiry date and require replacing once expired. Employers are responsible for identifying first aid equipment using appropriate safe condition signage (see page 23 and Figure 1.52).

A first-aider is someone who has received formal training and gained a recognised HSE-approved qualification in first aid. Two of the main first aid qualifications are Emergency First Aid at Work (EFAW) and First Aid at Work (FAW), with the latter being the more in-depth. These must be issued by an approved training organisation or awarding body. First aid advice does change from time to time and first-aiders are required to keep their qualification up to date with periodic refresher courses. Typically qualifications are valid for 3 years after which a refresher course is required to keep them current.

Companies generally keep a list of qualified first-aiders and have a rota of who is 'on duty' at any time. They may be called upon at any point to assist in an emergency. The number of designated first-aiders a company has available will depend upon the size of the company and the nature of the activities that they carry out. In a low risk environment the recommendation is one first-aider to every 100 employees. In a higher risk environment (such as an engineering context) a minimum of one first-aider to every 50 workers is required. Many organisations choose to exceed this number for extra security in case of absence/sickness. Very high risk activities may have additional first aid requirements and this would be included in the risk assessment.

Did you know?

First aid is everyone's responsibility. You need to make sure the first aid box is fully stocked. If you use, for example, the last plasters, report it to your line manager for restocking.

Practical first aid advice

Students often have mixed feelings about learning first aid. But if a family member, friend, colleague or a complete stranger needed your help, wouldn't you like to think that you could at least have a go at helping them? The information provided in this book is in no way a substitute for formal first aid training delivered by a qualified instructor. It is highly recommended that all engineers have at least a basic level of formal first aid training due to the higher risk industry in which they work. Below is some general advice on dealing with common first aid scenarios in engineering. But, we stress again, this is useful information only and *not* a first aid course in itself.

Wounds and bleeding

Small cuts and grazes should be treated by careful cleaning followed by a suitable sterile dressing. Remember that when skin is broken it is not only a route for blood to get out, but also for infection to get in. Therefore, cleanliness is very important – especially if it has occurred in a dirty engineering environment.

Blood is constantly pumped around the body, carrying oxygen to the vital organs. It is essential to the operation of our bodies and if we lose too much blood it can cause all sorts of problems. When dealing with cases of severe bleeding it is essential to reduce the loss of blood as soon as possible.

Below are some basic steps to achieve this.

* Clean disposable gloves should always be worn when dealing with cases of severe bleeding as a basic form of infection control.
* Apply pressure directly to the wound preferably using a sterile dressing/pad.
* Elevate the wound above the heart. It may be convenient to seat or lie the casualty down to achieve this (this action is also useful in case the victim falls unconscious to avoid them sustaining further injury).
* If foreign bodies are still present never try to remove them as they may be acting as a 'plug'. Apply pressure either side of the object and pack carefully when bandaging so as not to let it penetrate further.

- Bandage securely but not tightly enough to cut off blood supply to the affected limb.
- If blood seeps through the first bandage, apply a second over the top of the first. If the second bandage becomes saturated replace both but leave the dressing in place.
- Blood loss and the related trauma often results in shock, which should be treated as described below.

If amputation has occurred, treat the open wound primarily. If possible, find the amputated body part, wrap it in a clean dressing and pack it in with ice to be transported to hospital with the casualty. Never pack an amputated body part directly with ice as this can damage it further and reduce the chances of it being successfully re-attached.

Burns

When dealing with burns the key is to act fast to cool down the affected part and minimise severity. Run the burned area under water for a minimum of 10 minutes or until the burning stops. In the case of large areas a shower or bath may be used. Burns can easily become infected so try to keep them clean at all times. If required, remove jewellery and clothing from the affected area and cover gently with non-fluffy dressings that will not stick to the damaged skin. Clingfilm or plastic bags are recommended for this purpose! Any minor burns larger than the size of a postage stamp require medical attention – as do all deep burns.

Broken bones

Bones can be broken or fractured either completely or incompletely. Signs of a fracture include pain, swelling, deformity and loss of or unusual movement in a limb. Try to support and immobilise the affected limb to stop it from moving then treat for associated shock. Severe fractures may also be open or penetrating – where bones pierce through the skin. In this case treatment should also be given for the wound. Even with no external bleeding, internal injuries can have occurred, which can be very dangerous and medical advice should always be sought.

Eye damage

The eyes are very sensitive organs and when damaged require specialist attention. Ingress of liquids or tiny particles such as dust may be rinsed out using the sterile solutions found in first aid kits and eye wash stations. It is always best to get medical advice even for seemingly minor eye accidents. Anything larger or penetrating the eye should not be removed or touched. Gently place an eye pad over the eye and send the casualty to hospital as soon as possible.

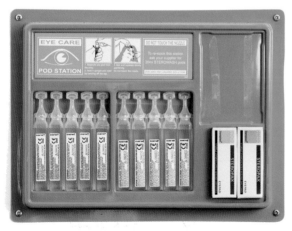

Figure 1.53 A typical eye wash station

Poisoning

Engineers often work with substances that can cause harm if accidentally swallowed, inhaled or absorbed through the skin; this is known as poisoning. How you deal with any particular toxin differs greatly. Refer to the material safety sheet for advice and seek medical attention as soon as possible. Always write down the name of the suspected poison or bring the safety sheet or container to hospital so that the staff can use this information to choose the best plan of action.

Shock

When the vital organs are not receiving enough oxygen the body can go into the condition known as shock. Shock can be caused by many factors including blood loss, heart attack, fluid loss and burns. Signs of someone going into shock include pale, cold clammy skin and fast rapid breathing and/or pulse. To treat for shock, firstly you should focus on what has caused the shock and treat accordingly. Lay the casualty on the floor and raise their legs, supporting them on a chair/box/books or whatever you have available. Loosen clothing, keep them warm and reassure the victim. Seek help.

Recovery position

When a victim is unconscious but breathing and has no other injuries they should be placed in the recovery position. The recovery position is designed to keep a casualty in a safe position; helping to keep their airway open and keeping them comfortable. In fact, the recovery position saves more lives than any other first aid procedure.

2. Gently roll person onto their side.

4. Tilt head back and tuck hand under chin to keep mouth open.

3. Bend leg to support position.

1. Bend arm to stop person rolling over.

5. Make sure someone is keeping an eye on them.

Figure 1.54 Steps to the recovery position

Hands On

Using some old first aid equipment, try out some basic techniques using role play. Working in a group of three, one person can pretend to be the casualty, one the first-aider and the third should act as an assessor, watching carefully and providing feedback at the end. Try to decide upon a scenario before the first-aider arrives and see if they act appropriately when walking into an unknown situation. Switch around so that each member of the group tries out each role.

Cardiopulmonary resuscitation (CPR)

Advice on how to carry out CPR effectively does change from time to time as new research on the subject comes to light. The following description is based on the Resuscitation Council UK 2010 resuscitation guidelines. It is always best to practise CPR with a trained first aid instructor using a model or mannequin; never attempt to practise on another person.

1. Assess the scene and make safe

Before approaching an unconscious victim assess the surroundings to make sure that it is safe to do so. If necessary take action to make safe the area, e.g. pressing emergency stops, removing hazards, clearing bystanders etc.

2. Assess consciousness

Check for responsiveness by gently shaking the shoulders and asking for a response loudly.

If the victim responds, continue standard first aid procedures leaving them where they are (as long as they are in a safe place) but continue to re-assess them periodically in case their situation worsens.

If the victim does not respond, continue as follows.

3. Call for help

If you are with others ask them to get help, for example summoning the appointed first-aider and/or assisting you. If you are by yourself shout clearly for help to attract attention.

4. Assess breathing

Position the victim on to their back and open their airway by carefully tilting the head back and lifting the chin. Check for normal breathing by listening, watching the chest rise and fall or feeling air on your cheek. Short, noisy, gasping or infrequent breaths are not normal breathing.

If the casualty is breathing, move them in to the recovery position (refer to page 39) and re-assess periodically. Otherwise continue below.

5. Call an ambulance

If others are with you ask them to call for help and (if available) bring an AED (see page 41).

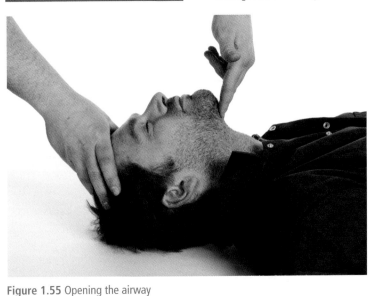

Figure 1.55 Opening the airway

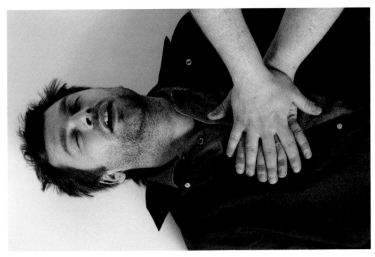

Figure 1.56 Chest compression

6. Begin chest compressions

You should carry out 30 chest compressions as follows.

Kneel by the side of the casualty with arms locked out and fingers interlocked. Push down firmly on the centre of the chest about 5–6 cm and release, at a rate of two a second.

7. Give rescue breaths

Give two rescue breaths by opening the airway, pinching the nose and breathing steadily into the casualties mouth. Allow the chest to fall before giving a second breath.

8. Repeat

Without any delay, return to your chest compressions – continuing in a 30:2 ratio as before. Only stop if the casualty recovers, help arrives or you are exhausted.

Delivering CPR is hard work and you will tire easily. Therefore, if possible, work with another first-aider – switching without delay every couple of minutes.

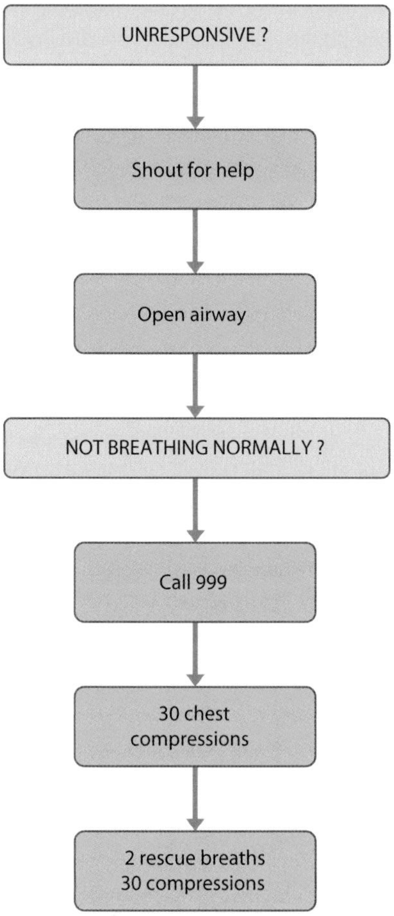

Notes on rescue breaths

If you are unwilling or unable to give rescue breaths, simply giving chest compressions can be effective by itself.

Face shields or masks included in some first aid kits can help with giving rescue breaths while offering some hygiene protection to the first-aider.

If the casualty vomits, turn them to the side and try to clear any vomit from their mouth/airway, then return to CPR.

UNRESPONSIVE ?

↓

Shout for help

↓

Open airway

↓

NOT BREATHING NORMALLY ?

↓

Call 999

↓

30 chest compressions

↓

2 rescue breaths 30 compressions

Figure 1.57 A CPR flow chart

Hands On

Talk to your employer or get in touch with St John Ambulance and get booked on to a formal first aid course. It is an essential life skill for an engineer and looks good on your CV.

Automated external defibrillators (AED)

Many public and work places now keep an automated external defibrillator (AED) which may be used during CPR. AEDs are very special computer-controlled devices that monitor a casualty's heart and can deliver electric shocks to attempt to make the heart regain its normal rhythm. AEDs give clear visual instructions and many speak out loud instructional steps when in use. They are designed to be used safely and effectively by an untrained or inexperienced user, although training is recommended. The unit carefully monitors a casualty and will not deliver a potentially damaging shock to a recipient who does not require it. It is important to remember that an AED does not simply replace CPR – it is used to supplement it.

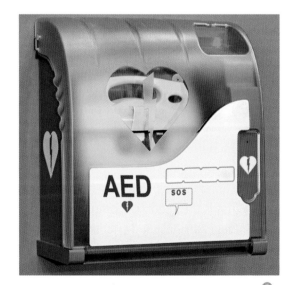

Figure 1.58 A typical AED

Calling an ambulance

In an emergency it is important to get the right professional help as soon as possible. Organisations often have a policy for how to contact the emergency services. For example, many like to have a central point of contact, e.g. reception, that is able to call 999 as well as organise internal personnel to act. This might include dispatching first-aiders, issuing first aid equipment and organising staff to direct arriving emergency services vehicles and personnel. For this reason it is a personal responsibility that you are aware of the appropriate way to act in this situation (see also emergency procedures page 17).

If you are in a situation where you need to call 999 here is some practical advice on how to act:

- stay calm and try to be as clear as possible
- listen to the emergency operator and answer their questions
- be aware that an emergency operator can dispatch help immediately but may continue to collect more information from you. This does not hold up help arriving
- if you are not using your own phone, try to have the phone number to hand. The operator may take this down to use it to call you back if there is a disconnection
- always remember that emergency operators are highly trained and experienced and they are there to help you. Treat them with respect and follow their instructions.

Hands On

Find out what the policy is at your place of work or school/college in terms of calling 999. Who is your area's designated first-aider and how would you get help in a medical emergency?

QUICK CHECK

1 What are the responsibilities of an employer in terms of first aid?
2 How many first-aiders would typically be required in these scenarios? Justify your answer.
   (a) an office block with 300 employees
   (b) a manufacturing company with 100 employees.
3 Describe what action you would take for:
   (a) a burn
   (b) a severe cut
   (c) an unconscious but breathing casualty.
4 What is the ration of compressions to breaths for standard CPR?
5 What is an AED and why are they so important? Who should use one?

INDUSTRY FOCUS

Helen is the Health and Safety Officer at an engineering company which uses a range of machinery and equipment to make consumer products.

'Health and safety is often misunderstood – it's not just all about paperwork – it's about making sure that the company looks after its employees so that we can work safely and do a really good job. I think that the job I do is really important.'

'I have to keep up to date with all of the constantly changing legislation to make sure that we are doing the right thing. One part of the job that I really like is when I have to teach others about health and safety. I think they expect me to be a boring nerd – but when I make learning about health and safety fun they soon see that I'm an engineer too and I'm just interested in taking care of them!'

'When a new piece of equipment comes in or we have to do a job differently I am in charge of looking in to how we go about things safely. This might involve talking to various people to help write a risk assessment and put in place proper control measures to make sure the activity is as safe as possible.'

'I often do "walk-arounds" where I visit all of the departments to see how they are working. Therefore, I get to work with lots of different people around the company making sure that they are all happy and – most importantly – safe.'

CHECK YOUR KNOWLEDGE

1 The Health and Safety at Work Act was passed in:
  a 1992
  b 1974
  c 1981
  d 2000

2 PPE stands for:
  a Protecting Personnel Effectively
  b Protective Personal Effects
  c Personal Protective Equipment
  d Practical Protection Equipment

3 A triangular sign with a yellow background and black pictogram indicates:
  a a potential hazard
  b something that must be done
  c something to do with fire
  d the position of a first aid box

4 A CO_2 extinguisher has what colour band?
  a Black
  b Blue
  c Cream
  d Red

5 In CPR, the correct ratio of chest compressions to breaths is:
  a 1:1
  b 10:1
  c 15:2
  d 30:2

6 Which of the following signs would not be green in colour?
  a Fire exit
  b First aid box
  c Fire extinguisher
  d Evacuation point

7 Which of the following is not required to start a fire?
  a CO_2
  b Fuel
  c Heat
  d Oxygen

8 According to the Workplace Health and Safety and Welfare Regulations the minimum working temperature for manual work is:
  a 16°C
  b 10°C
  c 13°C
  d 32°C

9 Which of the following is not an item of PPE?
  a Safety goggles
  b Face mask
  c Overalls
  d Machine guarding

10 In a workplace, who is responsible for maintaining health and safety?
  a The Health and Safety Executive
  b The employer
  c The employees
  d Everyone!

2 Working efficiently and effectively in engineering

This chapter will help you to develop the skills and competences that you need to start a career in engineering or manufacturing. It will help you to bridge the gap between college and employment and provide you with a range of new skills that you will help you at work.

Starting a new job can be very daunting and you will soon find that, in addition to the engineering skills you have learned, you will also need to demonstrate a variety of other skills in order to be effective. The most important of these additional skills is to know how to work safely, complying with your duties and obligations under the Health and Safety at Work Act.

In addition to being able to show that you can work safely, you will need to demonstrate effective planning skills in relation to a wide range of engineering tasks. As an engineer you will rarely be working on your own and so being able to maintain good working relationships with other people is another essential requirement. In addition, you will need to be able to solve any problems that arise in the course of your work, seeking advice and support from colleagues and specialists as appropriate to the task. All of this will help you to improve your effectiveness at work and allow you to develop your own engineering competence.

In this chapter you will learn about:

- working safely
- planning
- work plans
- job cards and work instructions
- tools and equipment
- health and safety

- preparation
- dealing with problems
- maintaining effective working relationships
- personal training and development
- completing the job
- improving working procedures

Working safely

You need to work safely at all times because many engineering activities can be hazardous, as this first case study shows.

You have been given the job of replacing one of the main bearings on a large motor-driven pump. This means visiting the customer's site, examining and dismantling the pump and replacing the bearing according to the specific instruction taken from the pump's work plan. You will need to put into practice the skills you have learned.

The pump that you will be working on consists of three main components: the pump itself, the electric motor, and the chassis on which the pump and the electric motor are both mounted. In addition, there is some electrical control gear for starting and stopping the motor and protecting the supply in case a fault develops. All of this equipment is fitted into a fairly small space and since the pump and motor are heavy you will need to lift the motor away from the pump in order to access the drive shaft and its main bearing. This is a complex task and there are quite a few things that you need to do before you get started. However, first and foremost you will need to remind yourself about how and why you need to work safely.

As you will recall from Chapter 1, working safely means complying with health and safety legislation, regulations and other relevant guidelines. These are designed to ensure your own safety as well as that of other people around you and anyone else who might be affected by your work.

Figure 2.01 You will need to consider many factors before working on the pump

1. How do all of these factors affect the work that you will be doing on the pump?

2. What other hazards might be present?

Hands On

Describe the personal protective equipment that would be required when performing each of the following engineering activities:

1. Soldering components on a printed circuit board

2. Machining a block of metal

3. Welding the seam of a metal enclosure

4. Cutting a sheet of aluminium with a power guillotine.

Key terms

Risk assessment – a careful examination of what, in your work, could cause harm to people. This will allow you to weigh up whether enough precautions have been taken or whether more needs to be done to prevent harm

COSHH – Control of Substances Hazardous to Health (a law that requires employers to control substances that are hazardous to health). Typical substances that are hazardous to health include ferric chloride, acids of various types, and hydraulic fluid

As you know from Chapter 1, all of the hazards that we have just considered should already have been identified in a **risk assessment** that should already have been carried out. Any specific problems will have been identified as a result of the risk assessment and they should feature in the work instruction that you will be following (see Chapter 3, page 83). If there are any hazardous materials present then you will be able to refer to the relevant materials safety data sheet (MSDS) required by the **COSHH** regulations that we looked at in Chapter 1 on page 10. You will need to read all of this through very carefully and check that you *do* have the correct personal protective equipment and that all of it is in good condition.

Planning

In engineering, planning involves thinking about all of the stages that need to be gone through in order to achieve a specific aim or complete a specific task. Planning is not done on a haphazard basis but requires careful and sometimes extensive research. For an effective plan you need to begin by defining the goal which should be specific, realistic, achievable and easily measurable. You need to identify all the main issues which have to be addressed, including a review of the different processes and techniques that could be applied. Planning also involves identifying any problems or difficulties that might be encountered – for example, the cost of materials or the production of toxic waste.

Figure 2.02 A selection of LED devices

Assume that you have been given the task of testing a large batch of light emitting diodes (LED) with the aim of selecting only those that meet a given specification. What information would you need in order to plan this task?

First, you will need a data sheet for the LEDs that you have been asked to test. This will provide you with some useful information including the forward voltage and current consumed by the LEDs when operating according within the limits stated on the manufacturer's written specification.

Next you will need to obtain appropriate test instruments (in this case a voltmeter and a milliammeter) and check that they are within calibration. You will also need a DC power supply with a suitable output voltage and current rating. Because this operates from the AC mains supply you should check that it has been recently PAT tested.

Using the power supply and meters, you will need to construct a test jig in order to supply power to each LED in turn so that you can measure and record the forward voltage and current. When each LED is connected in the jig you can also check it for colour and light output. You will need to repeat this process for each LED in the batch, sorting them into

'go' and 'no-go' batches depending upon whether or not they comply with the specification. Finally, you will need to record your results, ensuring that the batch of out-of-specification LEDs are correctly marked and disposed of.

In this example, you arrived at your plan by answering a series of questions:

1. What am I being asked to do?
2. What measurements do I need to make?
3. What documentation and additional information do I require?
4. How will I go about making the measurements?
5. What additional equipment will I require?
6. How will I be able to identify a working device?
7. How will I record my results?
8. How can I review my testing procedure?

The importance of planning

Effective planning is essential for several reasons. First, it will help you to ensure that the activity goes right and is trouble-free from start to finish. There would be little point in making the measurements on the LEDs without first establishing what specification they need to comply with. Secondly, planning will help you to ensure that the tasks that make up an activity are performed in the correct sequence and without error. After all, there would be little point in making measurements without first checking that the test equipment was within calibration and not showing erroneous readings!

Planning should help to ensure that only the right tools and equipment are available and that they are in a fit condition for use. It will also help to minimise the time taken to perform the activity. This is important as it will also help to reduce the cost of doing it.

Planning can help to ensure that there is effective coordination between those involved with (or who are affected by) the activity. Failing to mark the out-of-specification LEDs could result in them being passed on to other people who might not be aware of their shortcomings. Clearly it is important for everyone to know what others are doing and planning can help to do this.

Finally, planning can help you to organise a job so that it is done safely and efficiently. Checking that the power supply has been PAT tested before use is an example of this.

To summarise, engineering activities need to be carefully planned before you can start work. Planning involves various steps including checking that you have:

- the right tools and equipment
- an adequate supply of the right materials and components
- enough time and skill available to carry out the activity
- the necessary documents, drawings and any other relevant information
- a suitable area in which to work
- the correct personal protective equipment.

Planning will help you to produce a work plan which will provide the essential information that you need in order to divide an activity into a number of individual tasks arranged in a logical sequence. Work plans should leave nothing to chance and need to be detailed as you will see from the next section.

> **Hands On**
>
> Think of an engineering activity that you have carried out recently. Make a list of each of the individual tasks that have contributed to this activity and list them in the order in which they were carried out.

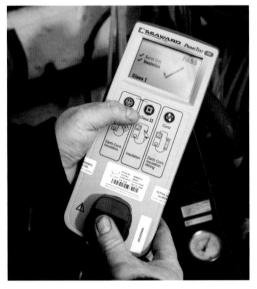

Figure 2.03 A PAT tester

QUICK CHECK

1 What is planning and why is it important?
2 List six steps in the planning of a typical engineering task.

Key terms

Activity – specific project that can usually be broken down into a series of tasks for example, to carry out a routine service on an engine. Activities are often performed in a set time (e.g. three hours to complete an engine service)

Tasks – the individual steps required to complete an activity. For example, when servicing an engine you would need to remove and replace the oil filter. Removing and replacing the oil filter is a task within an engine service activity

Work plans

When preparing for any engineering **activity** it is important to have a detailed work plan. But why are work plans important? Without them you might find that things go badly wrong. For example, you might forget to take an essential safety precaution or you might perform the task in the wrong sequence. It is important, for instance, to have the correct extractor to pull a bearing away from a driveshaft. Without it you might find it impossible to remove the bearing or you might damage the bearing by using an incorrect tool.

A work plan involves breaking down a complex engineering activity into a series of smaller **tasks**. Each task can then be described separately while the work plan shows how they relate to one another and specifies the sequence in which they need to be carried out.

Work plans are sometimes described using flow charts which give an overall view of the activity that is easy to understand. The flow chart shows the individual tasks that make up the activity as a series of boxes linked by arrows that indicate the sequence in which they need to be performed. A typical work plan for maintaining a pump is shown in Figure 2.04. Notice how this plan is divided into a series of tasks and each task can then be described in more detail.

From the work plan shown in Figure 2.04 you should see that it specifies:

- the individual maintenance tasks, their sequence, and any specific work instructions (see later) that provide detailed information relating to individual tasks where necessary
- the documents that you will need, including the exploded view drawing for the pump together with a detailed parts list
- the tools and equipment required, including electrical tester, torch, spanners, hexagon keys, mallet and screwdriver set
- the personal protective equipment (PPE) required to carry out each task.

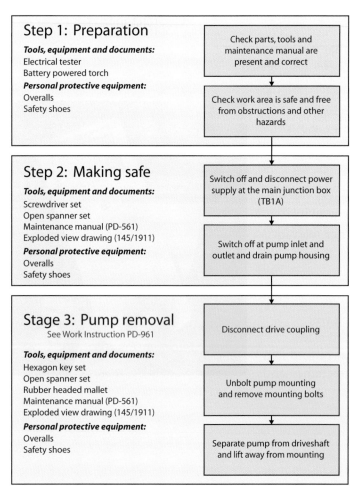

Step 1: Preparation

Tools, equipment and documents:
Electrical tester
Battery powered torch
Personal protective equipment:
Overalls
Safety shoes

> Check parts, tools and maintenance manual are present and correct

> Check work area is safe and free from obstructions and other hazards

Step 2: Making safe

Tools, equipment and documents:
Screwdriver set
Open spanner set
Maintenance manual (PD-561)
Exploded view drawing (145/1911)
Personal protective equipment:
Overalls
Safety shoes

> Switch off and disconnect power supply at the main junction box (TB1A)

> Switch off at pump inlet and outlet and drain pump housing

Stage 3: Pump removal
See Work Instruction PD-961

Tools, equipment and documents:
Hexagon key set
Open spanner set
Rubber headed mallet
Maintenance manual (PD-561)
Exploded view drawing (145/1911)
Personal protective equipment:
Overalls
Safety shoes

> Disconnect drive coupling

> Unbolt pump mounting and remove mounting bolts

> Separate pump from driveshaft and lift away from mounting

Figure 2.04 A work plan for the maintenance of a pump

Hands On

Devise a work plan for inspecting the brake pads on a motor vehicle. Make sure that your work plan is broken down into a series of tasks and that it includes a list of tools and equipment.

Job cards and work instructions

Job cards and work instructions provide you with detailed information on how to perform an engineering task.

Job cards

Job cards usually specify the following points.

- The title or job number of the task or activity – each task or activity must be uniquely identified so that it is not confused with any other task.
- The nature or brief description of the task and why it is needed.
- The location and date of the task and the name of the person responsible for carrying it out.
- The details of the task – this is often broken down into a series of sub-tasks.
- Details of any hazards and safety precautions that may be required in order to carry out the task.

TAYLOR AIR MAINTENANCE		JOB CARD		
Aircraft type: A340	Aircraft reg: SA-HBJ	Check interval: 1A	Job card number: 100951-01	Issue date: 2011-01-05

Warning:

PUT SAFETY DEVICES AND WARNING NOTICES IN POSITION BEFORE WORKING ON OR NEAR FLIGHT CONTROLS. CONTROL SURFACES, LANDING GEAR AND RELATED DOORS, ACTUATORS AND ALL OTHER MOVING COMPONENTS

Task:

1. MAKE SURE THAT GROUND SAFETY LOCKS ARE IN POSITION ON THE LANDING GEAR
2. INSPECT SIDE STAY BUSHES FOR CONDITION AND WEAR

Station: EASA 145 E-011	Inspection required? Yes [X] No [ ]	Critical task? Yes [X] No [ ]	Technician: *Alan Jones* Supervisor: *J. Wilson*	Date: 01-09-2011 Date: 01-09-2011

Figure 2.05 A job card for an aircraft maintenance task

Work instructions

Work instructions are more detailed than job cards and they usually specify the following points.

- The title of the task or activity – once again, each task or activity must be uniquely identified so that it is not confused with any other task.
- The details of the task – usually broken down into a series of sub-tasks.
- The parts and/or materials required to perform the task – these will normally be available from a parts store or may be supplied as a kit of parts for a particular task.
- The tools and equipment required to perform the task – specialised items of tooling, such as jigs and test fixtures may be required in some cases.
- The sequence in which the task is performed – this is important because some sub-tasks need to be completed before others can be started.
- Details of any hazards, safety precautions and PPE required – the job card or work instruction will normally assume that you are correctly dressed with suitable clothing and footwear so this will not normally be specified on the job card or work instruction.
- Relevant diagrams, drawings and sometimes photographs that illustrate the various stages in performing the task – work instructions normally contain more detail than job cards.

Hands On

Prepare a work instruction for an engineering task that you are familiar with. Make sure that your work instruction is sufficiently detailed and that it identifies any parts or materials required.

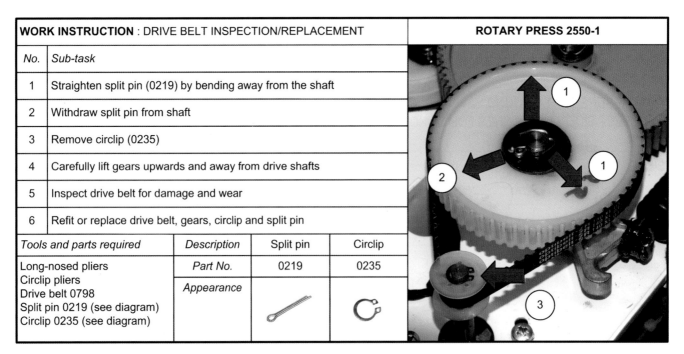

WORK INSTRUCTION : DRIVE BELT INSPECTION/REPLACEMENT				ROTARY PRESS 2550-1
No.	Sub-task			
1	Straighten split pin (0219) by bending away from the shaft			
2	Withdraw split pin from shaft			
3	Remove circlip (0235)			
4	Carefully lift gears upwards and away from drive shafts			
5	Inspect drive belt for damage and wear			
6	Refit or replace drive belt, gears, circlip and split pin			

Tools and parts required	Description	Split pin	Circlip
Long-nosed pliers	Part No.	0219	0235
Circlip pliers			
Drive belt 0798	Appearance		
Split pin 0219 (see diagram)			
Circlip 0235 (see diagram)			

Figure 2.06 A work instruction for the inspection and possible replacement of a drive belt in a rotary press

Using jobs cards and work instructions

Job cards are usually less detailed than work instructions. They often apply to a single task and include specific information, such as the location in which the task is to be performed, the time allocated for performing the task and the names of those responsible for carrying out the task. Work instructions act as an important record showing that a task has been performed and they are normally retained for tracking and billing purposes. Job cards are often used to record maintenance tasks while work instructions are normally used in engineering production and manufacturing. Typical job cards and work instructions are shown in Figures 2.05 and 2.06 respectively.

QUICK CHECK

1 What is a work plan and why would you need one?
2 List four things that you would expect to find in a work plan.
3 What is a work instruction and why would you need one?
4 How does a job card differ from a work instruction?
5 Why must a job card have a unique title or reference number?
6 List four things that you would expect to find in a typical work instruction.

Tools and equipment

When working as an engineer you will become familiar with a very wide range of tools and equipment; the most important of these will be described and explained in the technical chapters that follow. However, whatever branch of engineering you work in, it is really important to have the right tools and equipment needed to do the job. You will also find that, as you gain more experience, you can enjoy knowing how to make the best use of them.

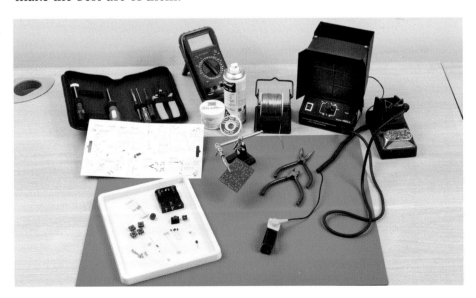

Figure 2.07 Tools laid out for inspection before carrying out an engineering task

Figure 2.08 Tools that are defective need to be clearly labelled so that they are not used by anyone else

Before carrying out a task you will need to check that each tool and item of equipment is present and in good condition before arranging them in the order in which they will be used. In most cases the work instruction or job card will help you select the right tools and equipment, but in some cases you will need to use your own skills to select the right tool or equipment to do the job.

You will need to make sure that each individual tool is safe, functional and in a usable condition. Any defects or problems, such as a loose handle or missing connector, should be reported to your immediate supervisor. Also ensure that any tool or equipment that you find defective is clearly marked and is not left for use by anyone else.

Case Study

As an example, assume that you are about to make a soldered connection between a cable and a connector. You would need to use a suitably rated soldering iron that was fitted with a bit of the correct shape. You would also need to ensure that the temperature was correctly set on the control unit and that the correct bit temperature was reached before attempting to make any soldered joints.

A brief examination of the soldering iron, cable and control unit should allow you to check and verify the following.

1. There is no external damage to the iron (particularly in the body/handle of the iron).

2. The bit is correctly fitted and not loose in its holder.

3. The cable linking the iron to the control unit is undamaged (in particular, you need to check that the insulation is intact and not nicked, damaged or burned).

4. Connectors are not loose, broken or damaged.

5. Indicators, switches and controls are undamaged and operate correctly.

6. The bit is cleaned and properly tinned.

Figure 2.09 A typical temperature controlled soldering station

Hands On

Prepare a checklist of the tools and equipment that you would need in order to remove and check a car battery.

Only the minimum of tools for the job should be laid out at any one time. They should be organised in a tidy and logical manner so that they are quickly and easily accessible.

Finally, it is very important **not** to begin a task or activity unless you have the correct tools and equipment. Avoid the temptation to use an incorrect or improper tool (such as using a screwdriver as a chisel!) as this may cause damage not only to the equipment that you are working on but also to the tool itself. Work instructions and job cards nearly always include a checklist of the tools and equipment that you need for a task so do make sure that you use it!

QUICK CHECK

1 What action should you take if you are issued with a tool or item of equipment that is defective?

2 List at least four checks that you would make before using a pillar drill to drill a series of small holes in a brass block.

Health and safety

In Chapter 1 you studied the roles and responsibilities of yourself and others under the Health and Safety at Work Act and you will also know what constitutes a hazard in the workplace. Table 2.01 shows these.

Hands On

Visit the Health and Safety Executive website at www.hse.gov.uk/coshh/basics.htm and use it to answer the following questions:

1. What is a 'substance hazardous to health'?

2. What are safety data sheets used for?

3. What is the purpose of a 'COSHH assessment'?

Situation	Possible hazard
Proximity of machinery with moving parts	Moving parts can get caught up in clothing
Use of electricity (particularly high voltages)	High voltages can cause electric shock
Presence of slippery and uneven surfaces	These can result in trips or falls
Presence of dust and fumes	These can cause irritation and respiratory problems
Lifting, handling and transportation of bulky and heavy items	Can lead to strains, muscular problems or material being dropped
Use of contaminants and irritants	On contact, these can cause irritation to exposed skin and eyes
Risk of fire and smoke	Can result in burns and suffocation
Equipment that operates at high pressure	Can cause injuries to exposed area
Risk of implosion and explosion	Flying debris that can cause cuts and bruises
Use of volatile and toxic materials	Result in irritation to skin and eyes as well as potential respiratory problems and poisoning

Table 2.01 Possible hazards in the workplace

Figure 2.10 Correct clothing for engineering work

Quick Tip

For many tasks and activities you will also need to obtain the required personal protective equipment (PPE) and ensure that it is usable.

Being able to recognise these hazards and avoid them is an important skill that must be acquired by anyone working as an engineer. Failure to recognise them can result in personal injury or in extreme cases permanent disability or death.

Health and safety guidelines

To ensure that you work safely you need to observe the following guidelines.

- Follow the procedures or systems in place for **risk assessment**, **COSHH**, **personal protective equipment** and other relevant safety regulations. For example, ensure that materials such as sheet metal are stored correctly.

- Wear personal protective equipment for the specific activity and work area in which it is being carried out. For example, wear gloves and eye protection when working with hazardous fluids such as ferric chloride etchant.

- Use tools and equipment safely and correctly, and only for their intended purpose. For example, use a rubber-headed mallet rather than a hammer to release a shaft from a bearing.

- Ensure that the work area is maintained and left in a safe and tidy condition. For example, remove accumulated swarf from the table of a milling machine after use.

- Wear appropriate clothing. For example, leather shoes or boots rather than trainers. Your clothes should be neat and clean and if you have long hair it should be tied back or netted. You will also need to remove any jewellery or other items that could become entangled in machinery.

Preparation

Preparation is important because it can save a lot of time and help you avoid problems later on. It can also help you to keep your work area safe. When you prepare for a work activity there are a number of things that you need to think about. First and foremost is to check and ensure that you have authorisation to carry out the work (some tasks, such as grinding, can only be performed by people who are properly qualified).

Next you will always need to make sure that your work area is free from hazards and is ready for the work that you are doing. You should check that the required safety procedures are implemented, referring to relevant safety documentation whenever necessary.

As mentioned earlier, you need to check that you have the correct tools, equipment, jigs and fixtures, checking that each item works properly and is safe to use. You will also need to ensure that you have the necessary work instructions and that you fully understand them before starting work. In addition to the work instructions you will need to have any relevant drawings, specifications and associated documents. These will usually be identified in the work instructions and should be available from your technical library or workshop bookshelf.

You will need to check that you have the right materials, components and parts required to carry out the job. Once again, these will be specified on the work instruction. Finally, it is worth summarising the steps just discussed in the form of a checklist:

1. Make sure that you have authorisation to carry out the work.
2. Make sure that your work area is free from hazards and is ready for the work that you are doing.
3. Check that the required safety procedures are implemented.
4. Obtain the required personal protective equipment (PPE) and ensure that it is usable.
5. Check that you have the correct tools and equipment and that everything works properly and is safe to use.
6. Make sure that you have the necessary work instructions and that you fully understand them.
7. Check that you have relevant drawings, specifications and associated documents.
8. Ensure that you have the correct materials, components and parts.

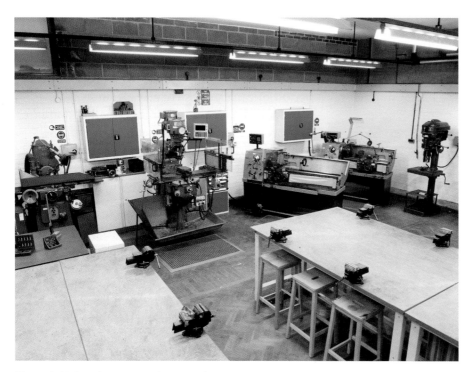

Figure 2.11 A work area correctly prepared

QUICK CHECK

Why is it important to **prepare** for an engineering activity? Give at least three reasons.

The work area

Is your work area safe and what things do you need to look for in order to create a work environment that is free from hazards? These are important questions and you should think about them carefully before starting work. A number of different factors need to be considered when creating a safe working area, including the need for adequate space, cleanliness, lighting and ventilation.

Space

When carrying out an engineering task it is important to think about how much space you need to do the work without the risk of harming yourself or others. Some engineering operations and processes require a considerable amount of clear space. Others may not be so demanding. For example, think about how much space you would need to change the wheels on a car. To carry out this task you would need a clear area on either side of the vehicle so that the jack could be fitted and operated and the wheel removed and replaced. You would be unable to change the wheels of a car if it was in a normal parking space with other vehicles parked either side!

The same considerations apply to all engineering tasks but, in addition, you should think about the proximity of other people and whether or not there is any risk that they could be in any way harmed by the work that you are doing.

Cleanliness

You should also check that the work area is clean and free from clutter, dust, dirt, offcuts and swarf. Clutter is simply materials, tools and equipment that have not been returned to the correct place. Clutter can be avoided by good 'housekeeping' – in other words, by clearing up after working. Dust is produced by many engineering processes and may accumulate over a period of time unless regular cleaning takes place. Dirt (including traces of oil and grease) is present in many engineering situations, particularly where equipment is used in environments that are not clean, such as a steelworks or quarry.

Offcuts are unwanted material that is left over after cutting. Offcuts can usually be recycled or retained for future use in tasks where less material is required. **Swarf** is shavings and chippings of metal left over from milling and grinding operations. Swarf can be sharp and so it needs requires careful handling. Swarf can usually be recycled following the removal of any leftover cutting fluid.

⚠ **Keep It Safe**

When welding you would need to ensure that other people were at a safe distance and could not be harmed by flames or flying sparks.

Figure 2.12 Typical swarf created during a machining process

Lighting

It is important to have sufficient light to see clearly the task that is being carried out. Failure to see properly can result in errors and wasted material. Within a work environment there is rarely enough natural light in order to carry out an engineering task. Instead, light must be produced by artificial means. This helps to avoid unwanted shadows and dark areas.

In some work areas several different forms of illumination are present. They may include overhead lighting to provide a general level of illumination together with bench or wall lamps to provide a higher level of illumination in a particular work area. In the case of electronic and other workshops where small parts are being used it may be necessary to use bench magnifiers which may also be fitted with a light source to aid close work.

Ventilation

The work area should be well ventilated. Some engineering activities, such as soldering, brazing and welding, produce dangerous fumes and specialised fume extraction equipment will be required. Remember that petrol and diesel engines produce fumes when they are running and so they should never be operated in a confined space.

Keep It Safe

Note that fluorescent lighting can result in stroboscopic effects when it is used to illuminate rotating machinery. This can sometimes be dangerous as it can give the illusion that rotating parts are running at a much slower speed than they really are.

Figure 2.13 Example of a well-lit work area in which plenty of space has been made available for the engineering tasks to be carried out

Hazardous materials

Within the immediate work area there should be no hazardous materials, such as acid and caustic substances, or flammable materials such as petrol, paint and solvents. These materials should always be clearly marked and stored in a safe place until they are required for use.

Electrical cables and hoses

Electrical cables and hoses should be carefully routed so that they will not get in the way or cause accidents due to fouling or tripping over. Cables and hoses should be clearly marked so that they can be seen and identified. After use, cables and hoses should be rolled up and stored. It is also important to make regular checks of the condition of hoses and cables. Any damage should be reported and the cable or hose in question should be removed from service and appropriately marked.

Noise and vibration

Noise and vibration produced by motorised equipment can often cause fatigue which in turn can reduce concentration. Loud noise can cause permanent damage to hearing and prolonged exposure can result in deafness. Vibration can cause nausea and prolonged exposure can be harmful to internal organs. Noise can be reduced by the use of acoustically absorbent enclosures while vibration can be reduced by using anti-vibration mountings. Both of these hazards can be minimised by appropriate workshop design and layout.

Fluid power equipment

Fluid power equipment can operate at high levels of pressure. Compressed air is often used as an alternative to electrical power in assembly areas while hydraulic fluid (a type of oil which is incompressible) is used to transmit power to the moving parts of machines. Escape of fluids can sometimes result in serious injuries and, since contact with hydraulic fluid can result in skin irritation and cancer, all fluid power equipment should be treated with the greatest respect. Hoses and joints should be regularly inspected and damage should be reported immediately.

Tidying up

Finally, it is important to always leave the work area clean and tidy and return all tools, equipment and any unused material or components to the appropriate place. Leaving the work area in a mess will make you extremely unpopular with colleagues and may even lead to an informal reprimand by your supervisor.

Keep It Safe

Electrical cables and hoses, if left out, can become slip and trip hazards.

Hands On

Think carefully about all the things you need to do *before* starting a particular engineering activity such as fabricating a metal enclosure or assembling a printed circuit board. Make a checklist list of everything that you would need to do before starting the task.

(a)

(b)

Figure 2.14 Examples of (a) a neat and tidy work area and (b) an untidy and dangerous work area

QUICK CHECK

1 List three hazardous substances that should not normally be found in an area where an engineering activity is taking place.
2 Why should petrol and diesel engines never be run in a confined space?
3 What is swarf? Why is swarf a problem and what should happen to it?
4 What problems can arise from noise and vibration and how can these problems be minimised?
5 Look at Figure 2.14(b) above. List ten examples of bad practice you can see in this image. What could you do to correct these?

Dealing with problems

As an engineer you will need to deal promptly and effectively with problems that are within your control. To solve other problems you will need to seek help and guidance from other people, such as your supervisor, line manager, or health and safety officer.

You may find that a tool that you are provided with is inadequate for the task that you have been given. This problem can be solved very easily by seeking the guidance of a more experienced colleague or referring it to your supervisor. Another example might be that you notice a defect in a component part. You can solve this problem by returning the part to the store and obtaining a replacement that is fully functional.

You will need to exercise judgement as to which problems you will be able to resolve on your own and which you will need to refer to other people. Problems that you might face include:

- the lack of specified materials, tools and equipment
- inadequate drawings and documentation
- the lack of sufficiently detailed work plans or job instructions
- damaged or defective parts, components and tools
- disagreements or lack of co-operation from other people
- not enough time to complete the task
- inadequate personal protective equipment
- unexpected safety hazards.

Sometimes it can be difficult to decide just how serious a problem is and in such a case you should always refer the matter to your supervisor and then follow his or her guidance. Three examples that might help you decide which problems you can solve by yourself and which need to be referred to other people are shown in Table 2.02.

Typical problems that you should be able to resolve on your own and the action you should take	Typical problems that you should refer to other people and who they should be referred to
You notice that you are using an outdated version of a general assembly drawing; take steps to obtain the latest version of the drawing	You notice that a safety warning sign has been removed from a machine; report this to your supervisor and/or safety officer
The display on your digital multimeter indicates that the battery is exhausted; return the multimeter to the equipment store, report the flat battery and obtain a replacement instrument	A fire exit has been obstructed; report this to your supervisor and/or safety officer
A visitor approaches you and tells you that he is lost; direct him to reception and telephone the receptionist to say that he is on his way	An electric cable has been damaged and one of the conductors has become exposed; switch off, disconnect the supply and report this to your supervisor

Table 2.02 Different problems in the workplace

People who can help

Many people will be able to help you with your work and you should not be afraid to ask them for help whenever you need it. Your supervisor or line manager is normally the first person to approach because he or she will have direct responsibility for you and for the work that you do.

Their main role is to ensure that you understand what it is that you need to do and to check that you are doing it correctly. They will oversee the work that you carry out, providing you with help and support when you need it. They will often inspect your work and provide you with feedback so that you can improve not only the way that you work but also the quality of the work that you do. You can learn a great deal from this feedback and should never be afraid to ask your supervisor to comment on your work.

Your colleagues and co-workers with whom you will have daily contact will often have more experience than you and may have a wide range of knowledge and skills that you can call on. You should avoid making too many demands on colleagues and, in some cases, it would be better to refer problems to your supervisor than to divert them from their own work. Because of your shared experience at work you will also find that you make friends with many of your colleagues. Such friendships can often last a lifetime so they can be really valuable.

Within any company there are a number of specialist roles. Some of these are shown in Table 2.03. These people all have clearly defined job roles which will usually be explained to you as part of your company induction. You should refer specific problems to them whenever the need arises.

Quick Tip

You will often get to know your supervisor or line manager quite well and they will usually be on hand to help you with any problems that you have.

Hands On

Think of one situation in which you have had to resolve a work-related problem on your own initiative and one situation when you have had to seek help and advice from others. What made these two situations different?

Job title	Description of role
Counsellor	Someone who is trained to give advice and support with any personal or emotional problems that you might have
First-aider	One or more people within a company or organisation who has received training in first aid. You will often find that one of your colleagues is a first-aider. They are usually the first person to contact whenever there is any accident involving personal injury
Payroll officer	Individual within a company or organisation who is responsible for ensuring that people are paid correctly and on time
Personnel officer or HR officer	Someone within a company or organisation who is responsible for all aspects of recruitment and employment within the company
Safety officer	Individual within a company or organisation who is responsible for all aspects of health and safety within the company
Training officer	A person within a company or organisation who is responsible for ensuring that people are correctly trained and prepared for the work that they do. In a small company the roles of personnel officer and training officer may be combined. In a large company they are usually separate roles
Union official	Within any large organisation there may be one or more trade unions that represent the interests of employees. Union officials are usually elected members of the union who can provide advice and support on issues relating to employment that cannot otherwise be solved by your supervisor or line manager

Table 2.03 Specialist roles

Did You Know

Most companies will give you an induction that will provide you with information about the company as well as who to contact if you have a problem. It is important to get the best out of your induction as it could save you a lot of time later on!

Quick Tip

When receiving instructions from other people it is important to check that you have understood everything. Do not be afraid to ask questions or seek further advice if there is anything that does not seem clear.

Giving and receiving instructions

Your supervisor or line manager will expect you to carry out instructions promptly. However, before you start work it is important to make sure that you have fully understood what you are being asked to do. Never be afraid to ask questions or seek clarification. Sometimes your supervisor will verbally tell you what to do. At other times your instructions will be written down in the form of a job card or work instruction. You should always ask for help or clarification if, after you have listened to or read your instructions carefully, there is something you still do not understand.

From time to time you might have to give instructions to someone else. If this happens you need to make sure that the instructions are given clearly and with the right amount of detail. Too much information that the person does not need will make the job more difficult; too little information and they will not be able to complete the job properly. Always ask if they have understood and make sure they can explain what it is they have been asked to do.

QUICK CHECK

1 What should you do immediately after giving an instruction to a colleague?
2 What is the difference between the role of payroll officer and personnel officer?
3 Who would be the first person to contact if you have a minor cut or bruise?

Maintaining effective working relationships

In engineering, as with any other work activity, it is essential to have good working relationships with colleagues and other people who you might have contact with in your day-to-day working life. Such relationships will not only help you to be effective in doing your own job but they will also allow others to be effective in their job roles.

Good working relationships are based on a positive attitude to work coupled with good communication skills and an ability to identify and respond to the needs of others. These skills can be easily acquired but they do involve you in being aware of what is going on around you and being willing and able to respond to the needs of others.

Few engineering activities are performed in complete isolation and all major engineering projects involve teamwork and co-operation. As you start your career in engineering you will inevitably become a member of a team and other people will depend on you – just as you depend on them. A good starting point is that of gaining the respect and support of those around you by listening to other people's needs and being prepared to give advice and support whenever necessary.

Hands On

Think of a task or activity where it would be essential to inform others about the work that you are carrying out because it may have an impact on their work. What would you need to do and why would you need to do it?

✓ Turn up at your workplace on time and suitably dressed for the work activities that you will be carrying out.

✓ Listen attentively, follow instructions and check out anything you are uncertain about before starting work.

✓ Seek information and help courteously and politely.

✓ Take advice from others in a positive way.

✓ Deal with disagreements amicably and constructively.

✓ Communicate with others nearby to make sure that they know about actions you are taking which may affect their work.

✓ Respond positively to requests for help from others.

✓ Be considerate and respect the rights, views and property of others.

Figure 2.15 Tips for working with others

Finally, do not forget that you need to be willing to give help and assistance to other people but if you cannot help or do not know the answer, say so. Make sure that you understand exactly what it is that you are being asked to do and, when you have provided help or given an answer, make sure that it has been understood.

Hands On

Why is teamwork important in engineering? Think of an engineering activity that needs a team in order to complete it. Why can't this activity be completed by just one engineer working in isolation?

Figure 2.16 Teamwork is an important part of engineering

Key terms

Legislation – a law or set of laws approved by Parliament

Equal opportunities legislation – legislation that provides a legal framework for implementing equal opportunities

Did You Know

The European Union is an economic and political union of 27 member states in Europe. The EU has developed a single market through a standard system of laws and regulations that apply in all member states.

Figure 2.17 Conformity mark for products produced in the European Union (EU)

Legislation and regulation

Some laws and regulations affect how people should be treated at work and you need to know how these govern what you can and cannot do at work. This **equal opportunities legislation** is shown in Table 2.04.

In addition, the Equality Act 2010 aims to end the discrimination that you might face if you belong to a group of people who may be less favourably treated than other people. For example, if you are gay or have a particular religious faith it is against the law to treat you in a way that will put you at a disadvantage.

Equal opportunities legislation	Description
The Equal Pay Act	A person has a right to the same pay and benefits as a person of the opposite sex in the same employment as long as a man and woman are doing exactly the same work
The Race Relations Act	It is against the law to discriminate against anyone on grounds of race, colour, nationality (including citizenship), or ethnic or national origin. It applies to jobs, training, housing, education and the provision of goods, facilities and services
The Sex Discrimination Act	Prohibits sex discrimination in employment, and education
Disability Discrimination Act	Aims to end the discrimination that many disabled people face. It gives disabled people new rights in terms of employment and access to goods, facilities and services, education and public transport
Equality Act	Strengthens and extends everyone's rights not to be discriminated against in all areas of life, including work

Table 2.04 Equal opportunities legislation

In addition, the Working Time Directive (not part of the equal opportunities legislation) limits the hours of work that an employee can be asked to do. It gives the right for workers in the European Union (EU) to a minimum number of holidays each year and at least 11 hours rest in any 24 hours' work. It also forbids excessive work at night and provides a right to work no more than 48 hours per week.

QUICK CHECK

1 What is equal opportunities legislation and why is it important?
2 What is the Working Time Directive and how does it affect the amount of work that you can be asked to do?
3 What is the aim of the Disability Discrimination Act and what rights does it convey?

Personal training and development

You will normally receive plenty of training for the work that you do. Some of the training that you receive will be for specific tasks or processes but some of it will be more general. In addition to the training that you receive, you will be expected to take responsibility for your own development within the job role that you have been allocated. You should be able to:

- describe what you need to know and the levels of skill and understanding needed to do your job
- describe your own training and development programme, what the objectives are and how your needs were identified
- keep track of progress towards your individual goals and objectives – are you on track and is it what you expected?
- use feedback and advice to improve your performance.

Continuous personal development is important because it will help you:

- to progress and realise your full potential
- define and achieve your goals and objectives
- acquire appropriate knowledge and skills
- enhance your career and improve your employability.

As part of your continuous personal development you will need to review your progress with your supervisor and/or training officer on a regular basis. This will help you to set goals and objectives by comparing your current level of skills, knowledge and understanding with those that you need to develop. Any shortfall can be identified and plans can be made for further training and development in order to put it right.

Finally, you need to remember that continuous personal development is your own responsibility. Other people, such as your supervisor or training officer, all have a role to play but ultimately it is you who must take charge of your own development. You will need to keep a formal record of your development on an ongoing basis, including evidence of your progress (such as date of the completion of any training or additional qualifications) and a clear statement of your goals and objectives and how they change over time.

Quick Tip

Always make sure that you keep your own training record and portfolio up to date whenever you finish an activity or complete an aspect of your training. Not only will this save you a lot of time but it will also ensure that everything you do is accurately recorded and available for later inspection.

Hands On

Think of a training activity or qualification that you successfully completed in the last 18 months. How did this contribute to your continuous personal development, how was it recorded and what evidence did you supply to show that you completed it?

Completing the job

The need to ensure that your work area is clean and tidy when you complete an activity has already been mentioned. In addition to this you will also need to:

- return tools and equipment to the proper place – usually a tool or equipment store
- return unused materials and components to the proper place – usually a material or part store
- return drawings, job cards and work instructions (and check that they are complete, clean and unmarked)
- dispose of waste materials in accordance with company procedures and environmental requirements
- complete all necessary documentation accurately and legibly
- identify, where appropriate, any damaged or unusable tools or equipment
- report any problems to your supervisor.

Waste materials

Many engineering activities produce waste materials. Sometimes these materials can be recycled after suitable processing. In other cases the materials need to be disposed of safely and in a way that is not harmful to the environment. Typical waste materials include:

- lubricants such as oil and grease
- solvents and other chemicals
- metal and plastic swarf.

Whenever you have to dispose of waste material it is essential that you follow the correct procedures laid down for use in your company. If you are in any way unsure about these you should speak to your supervisor.

Storage of tools and equipment

Tools and equipment should be stored in the right place; usually in a separate tool or equipment store where the space for each tool is clearly marked. All tools should be regularly checked and kept in good condition. Many companies use a check system in order to track the use of a particular tool or set of tools. You should make sure that you use this system, as it ensures that you always know where a tool is and whether it is being used or not.

Hands On

Investigate one waste material that is present in your workplace. What procedures are laid down for its disposal and what eventually happens to it?

Hands On

Explain where tools and equipment are stored and located in your workplace. Is there a check procedure for tools and equipment and if so how does it work?

Figure 2.18 A typical tool store

Hands On

Look at Figure 2.18 opposite. What examples of good practice can you see in this tool store? Is there anything you would do differently?

Figure 2.19 A storage for small parts

Hands On

Identify what small parts you use would require special storage. Are there any specific issues which might affect storage boxes like those shown in Figure 2.19?

QUICK CHECK

1   Name three different types of waste material that you will find in engineering.
2   What is the advantage of a check system for the issue of tools and equipment?
3   What should happen to a tool that is found to be defective?

Improving working procedures

As you gain experience you will find that you will become confident in the skills that you have gained. You will also find that you are in a position to advise and support others. This is an important aspect of being a team member and your company will encourage you to share your skills and knowledge with others. This will help to improve working practices and procedures. You should never be afraid to make useful suggestions that will help your company to be more efficient, more environmentally friendly, and more profitable.

There will usually be several ways in which you can put forward ideas. Some companies have a suggestion box in which ideas can be posted. Some companies even offer a reward for the best ideas! Others have regular team meetings in which ideas can be discussed. You might also find that your company provides gives you a regular **appraisal** with your supervisor. This will almost certainly provide you with an opportunity to comment on your work and suggest how it can be improved.

Here are just a few of the ways that you can make a positive contribution:

- suggest how working practices and methods can be improved
- identify problems that affect quality and suggest how they can be overcome
- suggest how tools and equipment can be better used
- suggest ways of improving internal communication
- identify training needs and development opportunities
- suggest ways of improving safety and avoiding hazards
- suggest modifications/improvements to products and services.

> **Key term**
>
> **Appraisal** – a meeting, usually involving just you and your supervisor, in which your work is reviewed. Many companies have an appraisal scheme that involves every employee in a regular review of his or her work. In some cases this is linked to pay or bonuses

QUICK CHECK

1 Why is it important to suggest ways of improving working practices and procedures?
2 Describe three different ways in which you can suggest ideas and make a positive contribution to working practices and procedures.

INDUSTRY FOCUS

In Formula 1 racing every second counts! The success of a Formula 1 racing team not only depends on every team member doing his or her job to the highest standard but also providing the best possible support for the rest of the team. Everyone needs to work together all of the time and this extends right through the team from the mechanics and technical specialists to the race engineer and the driver.

The continuous target of a racing team is to beat competitors by making their cars as fast and reliable as possible. This is the job of the technical team which comprises engineers, mechanics and other technical specialists. Without this team in place, even the fastest driver would never be successful. The most important link in the chain between the driver, car and technical team is the race engineer.

The race engineer's main role is to get the best from the car and the driver at the circuit. However, this is not their only job, as they have to communicate with the data analyst and mechanics, decide what changes to make and coordinate these as well. Away from the circuits, they must analyse the data from previous track times and make sure that the cars are ready for the next circuit.

The job of race engineer is extremely demanding and, because there is always a lot of pressure on the whole team to perform, a great deal of effort is required to maintain that same level of competitiveness. Being a good team member is essential; when there has been a major problem, mechanics and engineers might need to pull an 'all nighter' just to get the car ready for the next day.

CHECK YOUR KNOWLEDGE

1 Before you carry out a work activity it is essential to:

   a remove locks and guards from machinery

   b check that the work area is free from hazards

   c obtain a full set of manuals and equipment specifications

   d ensure that all windows and doors are closed and safety exits blocked

2 After completing a work activity it is necessary to:

   a leave unused materials and components in the work area

   b return tools and equipment to the designated location

   c make any necessary changes to drawings and other controlled documents

   d secure the work area by locking all doors, windows and safety exits

3 Which one of the following items is an example of personal protective equipment (PPE)?

   a Safety glasses

   b Laptop computer

   c Pocket calculator

   d Mobile phone

4 Which one of the following forms part of equal opportunities legislation?

   a The Health and Safety at Work Act

   b The Working Time Directive

   c The Disability Discrimination Act

   d The Personal Protective Equipment at Work Regulations

5 When you encounter a problem at work that you cannot solve on your own it is important to:

   a eliminate the problem by working round it

   b seek guidance and advice from your supervisor

   c make a note in your logbook for future reference

   d find another way of working that avoids the need to solve the problem

6 When given verbal instructions by your supervisor or line manager you should:

   a take notes so you can read them later on

   b listen carefully and make sure that you understand

   c chat and compare notes with the person next to you

   d ignore any detailed instructions as there's no need to remember them

7 Continuous personal development is important because:

   a it provides you with a break from work

   b it helps you identify problems at work

   c it helps you develop new skills and competences

   d it gives you an opportunity to forget what you've been doing

8 Working as a member of a team involves:

   a doing other people's work

   b solving problems on your own

   c working with other people to achieve a goal

   d checking that everyone does the same amount of work

9 Preparing for a work activity involves:

   a operating machinery and equipment

   b making sure that nobody else is around

   c checking that you have the right PPE for the job

   d tidying up the work that you have done previously

10 Good working relationships are based on:

   a an ability to work alone and not to involve other people

   b a need for constant supervision and the support of other people

   c an ability to amuse and distract people whenever a problem arises

   d a positive attitude to work and a willingness to work with other people

3

Using and communicating technical information

Being able to communicate information to other people quickly, clearly and accurately is an important engineering skill. This chapter will help you to select, use and interpret engineering information from a wide range of sources. It will also introduce you to the way that information is presented and how to make appropriate use of it.

As you work through this unit you will be expected to show that you can make appropriate use of information as a means of both informing and improving your own work as an engineer. You should be able to evaluate the information that you use in order to ensure that it is accurate, current and relevant.

In this unit you will learn about:

- engineering information
- application notes and technical reports
- data sheets and data books, including manuals
- quality documents
- specifications
- job cards and work instructions
- using and communicating technical information
- drawings and diagrams

- formal drawings
- drawing types and projections
- block diagrams and flow diagrams
- schematic diagrams
- using CAD
- assembly diagrams and exploded views
- charts, graphs and tables
- sources of data
- care and control of documents and drawings

Engineering information

Engineers need a variety of information to do their jobs; this can take various forms including written documents, diagrams and drawings. Being able to interpret this information and also being able to pass it on to other people is an essential skill that you will need to develop as you progress your career in engineering.

No matter what the form the information is in, it must be accurate, thorough, up to date and available when and where it is needed. In short, engineering information needs to be:

- accurate – the details needs to be correct and as precise as possible
- comprehensive – all of the necessary detail needs to be provided
- current – the information needs to be up to date
- accessible – the information should be available as and when required and in a form that makes it easy to use.

As an engineer you will seldom be working in isolation and you will nearly always work as a member of a team. You should, therefore, also be able to present information to others in a way that is clear and unambiguous, and in a manner that conforms to accepted codes of practice and standards.

Information sources

As an engineer you will need to locate appropriate sources of information, be able to extract relevant information from these sources and then be able to use it to solve real engineering problems.

Engineers get the information that they need to do their jobs from many different sources. Some information is presented in printed form (for example, reports and specifications) but increasingly it exists as **electronic data** that can be read on a screen or printed directly from a computer. Information is often presented visually in the form of drawings, diagrams and sketches. These can be stored as **hard-copy** printouts or as files stored on **digital media**.

Communication

Engineering information can be communicated in various ways, both formally and informally. Communication can take various different forms including:

- verbal – speaking
- non-verbal – body language, including gestures, facial expressions and body posture
- written – drawings and documents (including notes, memos, reports, job cards and work instructions)
- electronic communication – phone, email, Internet, text message, etc.

In engineering, everyday information is often given verbally, for example by spoken instructions. However, as with other forms of information,

---

Key terms

Electronic data – information that is encoded in digital form so that it can be processed and stored in a computer system

Hard copy – documents and drawings printed on paper

Digital media – documents and drawings typically stored on CD-ROMs, memory cards, USB memories, hard drives, and network servers it is often necessary to refer to additional information such as charts, tables and other reference data in order to obtain a full picture of what is needed.

In engineering it is important to have the right information for any job or task that you have to perform. When the job is finished (and also at certain stages of doing the job) you must be able to check that your work conforms to the specifications and quality standards that apply to it. Here again, it is important to have the information that you need, when you need it!

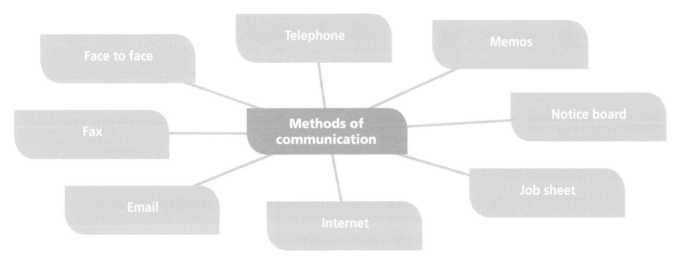

Figure 3.01 Different forms of engineering communication

Case Study

The Airbus A380 uses over four million parts and the aircraft's documentation refers to 2.5 million unique part numbers supplied by 1500 companies in 30 countries around the world. Some of these parts are very small and some are very large but they all need to work together to make the aircraft fly. Each part and each sub-assembly needs to be very accurately described and documented and keeping this information up to date is an essential task.

Visit the Airbus website at:

http://www.airbus.com/company/aircraft-manufacture/how-is-an-aircraft-built/

Use it to locate information on the manufacture of an Airbus aircraft and use it to answer the following questions:

Figure 3.02 Airbus A380 parts are made in 30 countries

1. Where does the final assembly of the A380 take place?

2. Following final assembly, what general tests are carried out on each aircraft?

3. What happens immediately before each aircraft flies for the first time?

QUICK CHECK

1 List three different ways in which information can be communicated.

2 List four key requirements for engineering information.

Application notes and technical reports

Engineering information often takes the form of written notes and reports. These are often supported by illustrations, diagrams and drawings.

Application notes

Application notes explain how something is used in a particular application or how it can be used to solve a particular problem. They are intended as a guide for designers and others who may be considering using a particular process or technology for the first time.

Application notes are usually brief notes (often equivalent in length to one of the chapters in this book) supplied by manufacturers in order to assist engineers and designers by providing typical examples of the use of parts and components.

Application notes can be very useful in providing practical information that can help designers to avoid pitfalls that might occur when using a component or device for the first time. They often include prototype schematics and layout diagrams and give sufficient information for engineers to build and test.

Technical reports

Technical reports are similar to application notes but they focus more on the performance specification of engineering components and devices (and the tests that have been carried out on them) than the practical aspects of their use. Technical reports usually include detailed specifications, graphs, charts and comparative data.

Technical reports provide information that is more to do with whether a component or device meets a particular specification or how it compares with other solutions. Technical reports are therefore more useful when analysing how a process or technology performs than how it is applied.

Typical section headings used in application notes and technical reports are described in Table 3.01.

Section header	Description
Summary	A brief overview for busy readers who need to quickly find out what the application note or technical report is about
Introduction	This sets the context and background and provides a brief description of the process or technology – why it is needed and what it does. It may also include a brief review of alternative methods and solutions
Main body	A comprehensive description of the process or technology
Evaluation	A detailed evaluation of the process or technology together with details of tests applied and measured performance specifications. In appropriate cases comparative performance specifications will be provided
Recommendations	This section provides information on how the process or technology should be implemented or deployed. It may include recommendations for storage or handling together with information relating to health and safety
Conclusions or summary	This section consists of a few concluding remarks
References and acknowledgments	This section provides readers with a list of sources for further information relating to the process or technology, including (where appropriate) relevant standards and legislation. It is also important to include the date, author's name, and contact information

Table 3.01 Typical section headers in application notes and technical reports

Case Study

The Global Positioning System (GPS) is a satellite-based navigation system made up of a network of 24 satellites placed into orbit by the US Department of Defense. GPS was originally intended for military applications, but in the 1980s the government made the system available for civilian use. GPS works in any weather conditions, anywhere in the world, 24 hours a day.

Use the Internet and/or other resources to investigate the operation of a simple GPS unit that can be fitted in a car. Write a brief summary (of no more than 750 words) that answers the following questions:

- How does the GPS system work?
- Where/how is it installed in a vehicle?
- How accurate is it?
- Are there any disadvantages of using GPS and how much does it cost?

Do not forget to include references and credit any sources that you used.

Figure 3.03 A car satnav uses GPS

QUICK CHECK

1 What would you expect to find in an application note?
2 Explain the difference between an application note and a technical report.
3 List five section headings that you would expect to find in a technical report.

Data sheets and data books, including manuals

Data sheets usually consist of abridged information on a particular engineering component or device. They usually provide maximum and minimum ratings, typical specifications, as well as information on dimensions, packaging and finish. Data sheets are usually supplied free

---

Linear wirewound potentiometers   14CF series

This low-cost range of 1W potentiometers are supplied in a bakelite case and use phenolic laminate formers. The standard 6.35 mm (¼ in.) spindle is plated brass and has a screwdriver slot to facilitate adjustment. Connecting terminals are silver plated brass.

Features:

- Compact
- Close tolerance
- 1W rating
- Long life

Applications:

- Power supplies
- Controllers
- General purpose

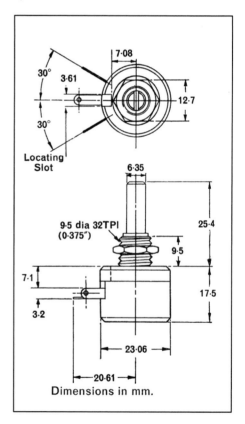

Dimensions in mm.

Specifications:

Range of values:	100Ω, 500Ω, 1kΩ, 5kΩ and 10kΩ
Tolerance:	5%
Power rating:	1W
Working voltage:	300V DC max.
Rotation:	275°
Starting torque:	360 gm. cm.
Working life:	>25,000 cycles
Insulation resistance:	>100MΩ at 500V DC

Figure 3.04 A datasheet for a wirewound potentiometer

on request from manufacturers and suppliers. Collections of data sheets for similar types of engineering components and devices are often supplied in book form. Often supplementary information is included relating to a complete family of products.

Catalogues

Most manufacturers and suppliers provide catalogues that list the range of products that they supply. These usually include part numbers, illustrations, brief specifications and prices. While catalogues are often extensive documents with many hundreds or thousands of pages, short-form catalogues are usually also available. These usually just list part numbers, brief descriptions and prices but rarely include any illustrations.

Catalogues and data sheets are often stored in electronic form and either made available for downloading from the Internet or distributed on a CD-ROM which can provide storage for around 700 Mb of data (equivalent to several thousand pages of printed A4 text and line diagrams).

Manuals

Various types of manual are associated with engineered products including:

> **Key term**
>
> **PDF** – a Portable Document File that can be read on wide range of electronic devices including desktop and laptop computers, tablets, and book readers

- user manuals or operating manuals – these are designed to be read by the end user of the product
- service manuals – these are designed to aid the repair and/or the routine maintenance of the product.

Manuals are usually produced by the company that has manufactured the product but may also be produced by third-party companies and organisations that specialise in producing them. Manuals are often supplied as booklets or leaflets but increasingly (for user convenience and also to reduce costs) they are being made available as **PDF** files available for download or supplied on a CD-ROM.

QUICK CHECK

1 What is a short-form catalogue and how does it differ from a full catalogue?
2 Why are catalogues and data sheets often stored in electronic form? Give at least two reasons.
3 What is the difference between a data sheet and an application note?
4 What is the difference between an operating manual and a service manual?

Howard Associates

54ALS08, 54AS08, 74ALS08, 74AS08
Quadruple 2-input AND gates

DATA SHEET

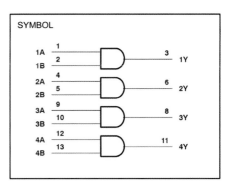

MAIN FEATURES

- Four independent 2-input positive logic AND gates
- Available in military (54) and commercial (74) versions
- Standard 14-pin DIL and 20-pin leadless packages
- Military version operates over a wide temperature range
- Complementary to 54/74ALS00 quad 2-input NAND gate

ABSOLUTE MAXIMUM RATINGS (T_A = +25°C)

Supply voltage, V_{CC}		7 V
Input voltage, V_I		7 V
Operating free-air temperature range, T_A:	54ALS08	−55°C to +125°C
	74ALS08	0°C to +70°C
Storage temperature, T_{stg}		−65°C to +150°C

TRUTH TABLE

INPUTS		OUTPUT
A	B	Y
H	H	H
L	X	L
X	L	L

H = logic 1 (high)
L = logic 0 (low)
X = don't care (either high or low)

ELECTRICAL CHARACTERISTICS (T_A = +25°C)

Parameter	Symbol	54ALS08			74ALS08			Unit
		Min.	Nom.	Max.	Min.	Nom.	Max.	
Supply voltage	V_{CC}	4.5	5.0	5.5	4.5	5.0	5.5	V
High-level input voltage	V_{IH}	2.0			2.0			V
Low-level input voltage	V_{IL}			0.8			0.8	V
High-level output current	I_{OH}			−0.4			−0.4	mA
Low-level output current	I_{OL}			4.0			8.0	mA
Operating free-air temperature	T_A	−55		125	0		70	°C

Data sheet reference: 95-072

© Howard Associates 2007

Figure 3.05 Data sheet for an integrated circuit

Hands On

Figure 3.05 shows a data sheet for an integrated circuit. Use the data sheet to answer the following questions:

1. What is the logic function of the device?
2. How many individual logic gates are available within the device?
3. What is lowest operating temperature for a 74ALS08 device?
4. What is the nominal supply voltage for a 54ALS08?
5. Which connecting pins are used for the supply voltage?

Quality documents

All engineering companies have **quality** systems in place to ensure that they produce goods and services of an appropriate quality. These systems are invariably based on formal documented procedures which usually include one or more of the following.

- **Quality procedures** – a detailed written description of the quality system and the controls that are in place within the company (these often form part of a quality manual).

- **Work instructions** – a description of a particular operation or task in terms of what must be done, who should do it, when it should be done and what materials and processes should be used. In many cases, a series of work instructions are used to describe each stage in the production or manufacturing process.

- **Specifications** – a detailed list of characteristics and features used to verify **conformance** with the design specification together with details of any measurements that are to be made out and how they should be carried out.

Documents are also used to assist in the process of identification and traceability of products, components and materials. This is vitally important in critical sectors such as aerospace, nuclear and chemical engineering where component failure can sometime have serious consequences. Traceability is essential when it becomes necessary to eliminate the causes of non-conformance. Traceability is achieved by coding items and maintaining records that can be updated throughout the working life of a component or record.

Key terms

Quality – a product or service should be 'free from defect' and will operate according to specification thus fully meeting the needs and expectations of clients or users

Conformance – confirmation that a product or service is able to satisfy or exceed a given specification. Conformance testing is often used to determine whether a product or service meets a specified standard or standards

Hands On

Visit the website of BSI at www.bsi-emea.com/Quality/Overview and then answer the following questions:

1. What is ISO 9000?

2. What are the main sections in ISO 9001:2000?

3. What steps should a company or business take in order to obtain the maximum benefit from ISO 9000:2000?

4. What would you expect to find in a Quality Manual?

QUICK CHECK

1 What is the purpose of a quality system?

2 What is traceability and why is it important in some industries?

Specifications

Written specifications should take the form of a precise and comprehensive description of the product. Specifications should relate not only to the physical characteristics and appearance of a product but also to the performance of a product in a way that can be measured in order to verify its performance.

Since specifications form the basis of a contract between a manufacturer or supplier and a client or customer, they need to be written in terms of what the purchaser requires and in clear, unambiguous words. There are three different types of specification.

- **General specifications** – detailed written description of the product including its appearance, construction, and materials used.
- **Performance specification** – a list of features of the product that contribute to its ability to meet the needs of the client or end user. For example, output voltage, power, or speed.
- **Standard specification** – describes the materials and processes (where appropriate) used in the manufacture of the product in terms of relevant standards (e.g. ISO 9000).

A typical performance specification for a power supply might be:

Input voltage:	110 to 220V AC 50 to 60Hz
Output voltage:	13.5V DC
Maximum load:	5A
Regulation:	Better than 2.5 % at full load
Weight:	1.5 kg
Dimensions:	155 × 85 × 65 mm
Connector:	Standard IEC
Compliance:	CE

Job cards and work instructions

Job cards and work instructions were described in Chapter 2 but since they are an important way of communicating engineering information we will mention them briefly in this new context.

Hands On

Obtain the technical specification for at least three portable electric drills from different manufacturers. Summarise these specifications in the form of a table with headings that include supply voltage, battery capacity, charging time, no-load speed, maximum torque and chuck size. Do any of the drills conform to recognised standards and, if so, what are they?

Figure 3.06 A portable electric drill

Job cards

Job cards provide information about parts and equipment and what should be done with them. They usually list the work that needs to be done and they may also include the time allocated for each task or sub-task. Job cards are often used when equipment is sent away for service or repair (see Figure 3.07) but they might also relate to a particular stage in the manufacture of a product.

Figure 3.07 A job card for a maintenance task to be carried out on a vehicle

Work instructions

Work instructions were described in Chapter 2 and they usually contain more detail than job cards. In particular they describe the individual stages of performing a particular task or sub-task. See Chapter 2 pages 52–53.

What to include in a work instruction depends on the complexity of the task, the skill level of the person carrying it out and also any regulatory requirements (such as might apply in the gas, petrochemical, nuclear and aviation industries).

When a task is more complex or when new unskilled workers are used, more detailed work instructions may be required. Modern work instructions are often 'paperless' and based on documents, drawings and photographs stored in electronic form on a networked computer system. This is particularly important when regulatory requirements require stringent reporting and revision control.

Did You Know

In many environments pictorial-based work instructions are used. These typically involve four to five steps described with only a small amount of detail but with a picture supporting each sub-task.

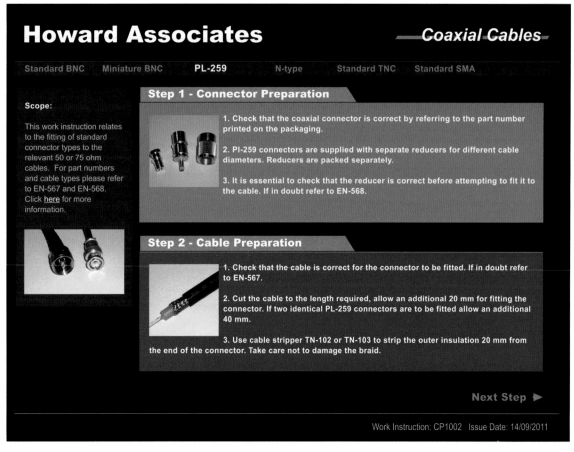

Howard Associates — *Coaxial Cables*

Standard BNC   Miniature BNC   **PL-259**   N-type   Standard TNC   Standard SMA

Scope:

This work instruction relates to the fitting of standard connector types to the relevant 50 or 75 ohm cables. For part numbers and cable types please refer to EN-567 and EN-568. Click here for more information.

Step 1 - Connector Preparation

1. Check that the coaxial connector is correct by referring to the part number printed on the packaging.

2. Pl-259 connectors are supplied with separate reducers for different cable diameters. Reducers are packed separately.

3. It is essential to check that the reducer is correct before attempting to fit it to the cable. If in doubt refer to EN-568.

Step 2 - Cable Preparation

1. Check that the cable is correct for the connector to be fitted. If in doubt refer to EN-567.

2. Cut the cable to the length required, allow an additional 20 mm for fitting the connector. If two identical PL-259 connectors are to be fitted allow an additional 40 mm.

3. Use cable stripper TN-102 or TN-103 to strip the outer insulation 20 mm from the end of the connector. Take care not to damage the braid.

Next Step ▶

Work Instruction: CP1002   Issue Date: 14/09/2011

Figure 3.08 A work instruction presented in electronic form for display on the screen of a tablet computer

Key terms

Tolerance – maximum deviation (i.e. difference) from the specified or nominal value. Tolerance may be expressed as a range of values (e.g. 25 +1.5/–0.2) or as a percentage (e.g. 15 ±10%). Closer or tighter tolerances are more difficult, and hence more costly, to achieve. Conversely, larger or looser tolerances may have an adverse affect on the operation and/or reliability of a product or system

Finish – one or more processes that are applied to a product in order to improve its appearance or to protect it from corrosion or abrasion. Finishing processes may also be used to improve adhesion or 'wettability', hardness and conductivity. They can also help to remove burrs and other surface flaws or control the surface friction

Using and communicating technical information

Engineering information can be communicated in various ways, both verbally and in written form. When communicating technical information you should ensure that you follow correct document care and control procedures and that you report any errors or inaccuracies in the drawings and specifications. You will also need to use the information obtained to establish work requirements, such as appropriate materials, **tolerances** and **finishes**.

In addition you will need to record and communicate the technical information by appropriate means such as:

- producing fully detailed sketches of work/circuits completed or required
- preparing work planning documentation
- recording data from testing activities
- producing technical reports on activities they have completed
- completing material and tool requisition documentation
- producing a list of replacement parts required for a maintenance activity
- completing training records or portfolio references.

List four ways in which engineering information can be communicated. Give an example of the use of each method.

Dealing with problems

You will need to deal promptly and effectively with any problems that arise and that are within your control. You will find that some of these problems can be solved quite easily without having to involve other people. However, to solve other problems you may have to seek help and guidance from other people.

Regular team meetings are held in many engineering companies and these can provide a useful forum for discussing problems and sharing ideas that can lead to a solution. More immediate and pressing problems may need to be resolved very quickly. These should normally be referred to your supervisor or team leader.

Figure 3.09 Accurate measurements are required in order to determine tolerances

Hands On

Which of these two problems could you expect to solve without help from other people and which would you need to seek guidance in order to solve? What would be the first thing that you would do in each situation?

1. You discover an error that relates to an incorrectly located component on a general arrangement drawing.

2. You are referring to a surface finish applied to a machined component and you discover that you are using an earlier version of a controlled drawing.

Drawings and diagrams

Engineers use many different kinds of diagram and drawing as a means of communication. The main reasons for this are as follows:

- diagrams and drawings can often convey information more clearly and easily than using words
- diagrams and drawings can contain extra information including dimensions and materials
- diagrams and drawings can provide different views of a component, sub-assembly or a complete product
- diagrams and drawings can show how component parts fit together to make a complete assembly.

As an engineer you must be able to read and use working drawings as well as producing your own sketches and diagrams. To avoid confusion your drawings must comply with recommended standards and conventions.

Key term

Projection – a way of drawing a 3D object by viewing it from different directions

Quick Tip

When making a sketch it is always best to use an HB pencil and an eraser rather than a ballpoint pen. Using a pencil and eraser makes it possible to easily remove any unwanted or incorrect lines. When complete you can always go over your pencil sketch using a permanent ink drawing pen.

The types of diagram and drawing that you need to be familiar with include:

- general arrangement (GA) drawings
- layout diagrams and exploded views
- block schematics and flow charts
- electrical and electronic circuit diagrams
- pneumatic and hydraulic circuit diagrams
- mechanical engineering drawings using various **projections**
- charts and graphs.

Informal and formal drawings

Depending on the way they are presented, drawings are often classified as either formal or informal. Informal drawings are usually sketches or hand-drawn diagrams that provide a quick impression of what something will look like or how something will work. Formal drawings (see Figure 3.10) generally take much longer to produce and usually contain a lot more detail. They are also much more precise and may include features such as a scale, dimensions, materials, finishes and a title block.

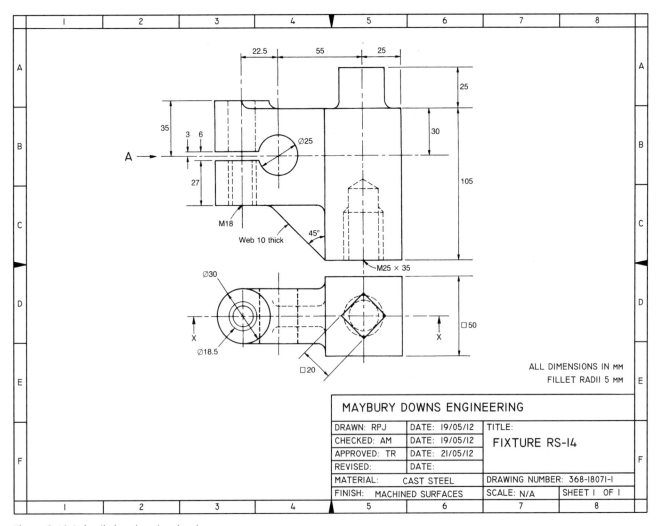

Figure 3.10 A detailed engineering drawing

Sketches

Sketching is one of the most useful tools available to the engineer to express their ideas and preliminary designs. Sketches are drawn freehand and they are used to gain a quick impression of what something will look like. A sketch can be either a two-dimensional (2D) representation or a three-dimensional (3D) representation (see Figure 3.11). A sketch can also be used to draw a block diagram or a schematic diagram (see pages 93 and 94). Labels, approximate dimensions and brief notes can be added to any of these types of drawing.

When producing a sketch you need to ensure that it is:

- clear and easy to read
- of suitable size – otherwise it might be difficult for others to read
- using the correct symbols and drawing conventions
- in proportion to the real part or component.

Failure to observe one or more of these considerations will at best make your sketch difficult to read and at worst may convey the wrong information.

Hands On

Produce a 3D sketch of an engineering tool, such as a machine vice, G-clamp, or adjustable spanner, that you are familiar with. Label your sketch clearly showing the individual parts that make up the tool and the materials of which they are made. Also add approximate dimensions on your sketch.

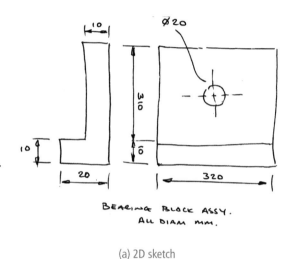

(a) 2D sketch

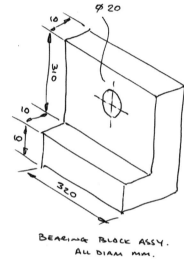

(b) 3D sketch

Figure 3.11 Simple 2D and 3D sketches

QUICK CHECK

1 What is the difference between a formal drawing and an informal drawing? What extra information would you expect to find in a formal drawing?
2 List four things that you need to take into account when making a sketch of a engineering part or component.

Formal drawings

Figure 3.12 shows the layout of a typical formal drawing. A formal engineering drawing should always have a border and a title block. So that individual features of a drawing can be easily located, the border often has letters along one axis and numbers along the other. It is thus possible to identify a particular drawing zone, for example C4 has been shaded in Figure 3.12.

To save time, most companies use a standard drawing sheet layout which is saved as a CAD template. Most CAD programs provide a selection of different drawing templates for different paper sizes.

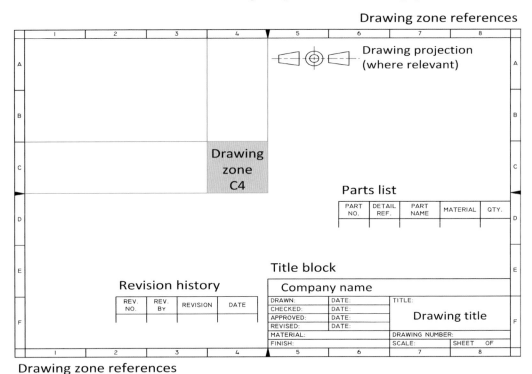

Figure 3.12 A company drawing sheet template

Title blocks

The title block (see Figure 3.12) can be expanded to accommodate any written information that is required. The title block will normally include:

- the company name and contact details
- the drawing name or title
- the drawing number (which is often repeated in the top left-hand corner of the drawing)
- the scale or dimensions used for the drawing (including scale ratio)
- the projection used (e.g. first or third angle)
- the name and signature of the person who made the drawing (i.e. the originator)
- the name and signature of the person who checks and/or approves the drawing, together with the date on which it was approved
- the drawing issue number and its release date
- the details of each revision made to the drawing (including who made the revision and when it was made)
- any other information (as appropriate).

In addition, a list of component parts may be provided (together with numbered references shown on the drawing), the materials that are to be used, the finish that is to be applied, the units used for measurement and tolerances, reference to appropriate standards (e.g. BS 8888) and guidance notes (such as 'do not scale').

When a scale is used this is normally stated on the drawing as a ratio. Frequently used scales are:

- full size, i.e. 1:1
- reduced scales (smaller than full size), e.g. 1:2, 1:5, 1:10, 1:20, 1:50, 1:100, etc.)
- enlarged scales (larger than full size), e.g. 2:1, 5:1, 10:1, 20:1, 50:1, 100:1, etc.).

General arrangement (GA) drawings

Figure 3.13 shows a typical general arrangement (GA) drawing. This shows as many of the features listed above as are appropriate for this drawing. It shows all the components correctly assembled together. Dimensions are not usually given on GA drawings although, sometimes, overall dimensions will be given for reference when the GA drawing is of a large assembly drawn to a reduced scale.

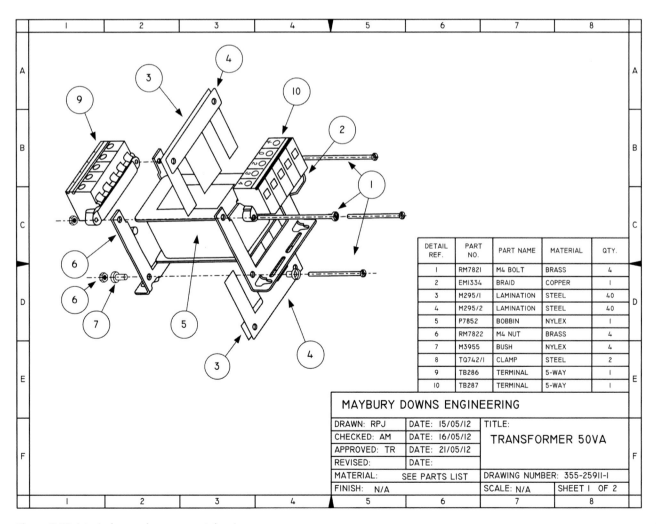

DETAIL REF.	PART NO.	PART NAME	MATERIAL	QTY.
I	RM7821	M4 BOLT	BRASS	4
2	EMI334	BRAID	COPPER	I
3	M295/I	LAMINATION	STEEL	40
4	M295/2	LAMINATION	STEEL	40
5	P7852	BOBBIN	NYLEX	I
6	RM7822	M4 NUT	BRASS	4
7	M3955	BUSH	NYLEX	4
8	TQ742/I	CLAMP	STEEL	2
9	TB286	TERMINAL	5-WAY	I
10	TB287	TERMINAL	5-WAY	I

MAYBURY DOWNS ENGINEERING

DRAWN: RPJ	DATE: 15/05/12	TITLE:
CHECKED: AM	DATE: 16/05/12	**TRANSFORMER 50VA**
APPROVED: TR	DATE: 21/05/12	
REVISED:	DATE:	
MATERIAL:	SEE PARTS LIST	DRAWING NUMBER: 355-259II-I
FINISH: N/A		SCALE: N/A	SHEET I OF 2

Figure 3.13 A typical general arrangement drawing

The GA drawing shows all the parts used in an assembly. These are often listed in a table together with the quantities required. Manufacturers' catalogue references are also given for any components that are not actually being manufactured. The parts are usually bought-in as off-the-shelf parts from other suppliers. The detail drawing numbers are also included for components that have to be manufactured as special items.

Detail drawings

Detail drawings like the one shown in Figure 3.10 on page 86 provide all the information needed to make a particular part or component. They usually include dimensions and tolerances as well as details of any finishes that need to be applied. The amount of information given in a detail drawing depends very much on the complexity of the job. For example, drawings for a critical aircraft component need to be much more detailed than those for a garden tool.

Dimensions

When dimensions are to be included in a drawing or sketch they need to be added in a way that aids the interpretation of the drawing and does not cause confusion or misinterpretation. Dimensions need to be added in a way that:

- closely follows the conventions associated with dimensioning
- cannot be confused with the original drawing lines and annotation
- uses a common fixed reference point.

Hands On

Figure 3.13 shows a dimensioned drawing of a part.

- What are the overall dimensions (length and width) of the part?
- What is the distance of the centre of the hole from each of the part's edges?

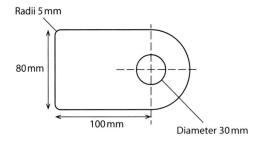

Figure 3.14 A dimensioned drawing of a part

QUICK CHECK

1 What is the difference between a reduced scale and an enlarged scale on an engineering drawing?
2 What is the difference between a general arrangement (GA) drawing and a detail drawing? How are these two types of drawing related?
3 What information would you expect to find in the title block of a formal drawing? Explain why this information is important.

Drawing types and projections

Engineering drawings such as general arrangement (GA) drawings and detail drawings that you have already met are produced by a technique called orthographic drawing. This represents a three-dimensional solid object on the two-dimensional surface of a sheet of drawing paper. It is drawn so that all the dimensions are true length and all the surfaces are true shape. To achieve this when surfaces are inclined to the vertical or the horizontal auxiliary views are used, but more about these later.

Isometric drawings

Isometric drawings allow us to show three-dimensional objects by drawing vertical lines conventionally and all other lines drawn at an angle of 30° to the horizontal, as shown in Figure 3.15. Lines are normally drawn using their correct (or correctly scaled) length. Modern CAD systems (see below) make this easy by helping to snap lines to an isometric grid and also by drawing ellipses to represent circles.

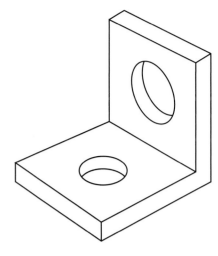

Figure 3.15 An isometric drawing

First angle projection

When it is necessary to show an object in more detail it is necessary to show a series of views taken from different directions. Two methods are commonly used, first angle and third angle projection. First angle is sometimes called 'English projection' while third angle is called 'American projection'.

In the case of first angle projection the drawing starts with a front view of the object and then, by looking from one side of the object you draw what you would see on the other side. Next you look at the object from above and draw what you would see underneath. Figure 3.16 shows how this is done but, to summarise, here are how the three individual views are produced.

> **Hands On**
>
> Use manual drawing techniques to create a first angle orthographic drawing of a simple engineering part such as a flange or bracket. Make sure that you correctly show all three views of the part.

- **Front elevation** – this is the main view from which all the other views are positioned. You look directly at the part and draw what you see.
- **End elevation** – to draw this you look directly at the side of the part and draw what you see *at the opposite side*. Note that, for some parts you might need two end views, one at each side of the elevation.
- **Plan** – to draw this, you look directly down on the top of the part and draw what you see below the elevation.

Figure 3.16 requires only one end view. When there is only one end view this can be placed at either end of the elevation, depending on which position gives the greater clarity and ease of interpretation.

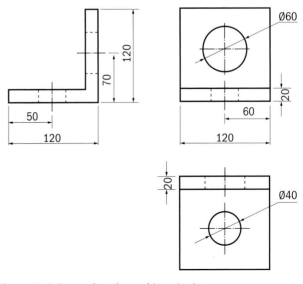

Figure 3.16 First angle orthographic projection

Third angle projection

In the case of third angle projection the drawing once again starts with a front view of the object but this time you look at one side of the object and draw what you would see on the *same* side. Next you look at the object from above and draw what you would see from the above (*not* from underneath as was the case with first angle projection). Figure 3.17 shows how this appears. Once again, here are how the three individual views are produced.

- **Front elevation** – this is the main view from which all the other views are positioned. You look directly at the part and draw what you see.
- **End elevation** – to draw this you look directly at the side of the part and again draw what you see. As before, it is worth noting that, for some parts, you might need two end views, one at each end of the elevation.
- **Plan** – to draw this, you look directly down on the top of the part and draw what you see below the elevation.

Once again, Figure 3.17 shows a simple part and this only requires one end view.

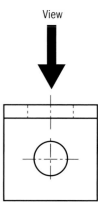

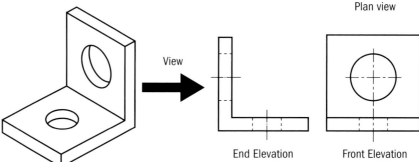

Figure 3.17 Third angle orthographic projection

Auxiliary views

In addition to the main views shown on a drawing sheet we sometimes have to use auxiliary views in order to clarify the drawing and reduce ambiguity. We use auxiliary views when we cannot show the true outline of the component or when we wish to illustrate a particular feature of the component.

QUICK CHECK

1 What is isometric projection and why is it used?
2 What is the difference between first angle and third angle projection? Which method is commonly used in the UK and which is commonly used in the USA?

Block diagrams and flow diagrams

Block and flow diagrams are often used in engineering to show how parts or processes are linked together. They provide a simple visual representation of a process or system that is very easy to understand.

Block diagrams

Block diagrams are useful for showing how individual parts are connected or linked together. They are not intended to show the physical relationship between the parts but instead they show how the parts are interconnected. Block diagrams use shapes (often square or rectangular boxes connected together with arrowed lines to show the flow of signals, power, fluid or information). Figure 3.18 shows the block diagram of the electronic control unit (ECU) used with a diesel engine. Diagrams like this can be very useful when carrying out fault finding.

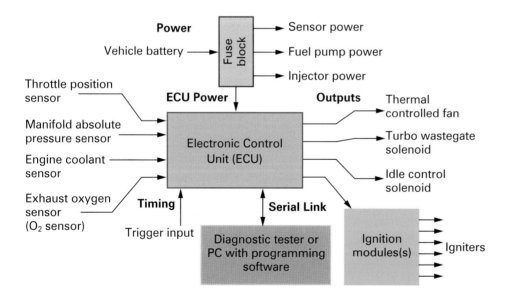

Figure 3.18 A block schematic diagram for an electronic control unit (ECU)

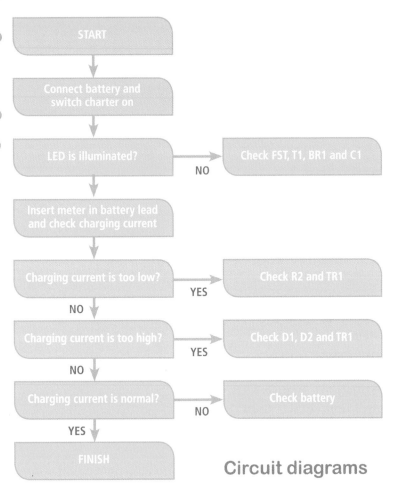

Figure 3.19 Flow chart for fault-finding on a battery charger

Hands On

Sketch a flow chart to illustrate the process of transferring images from a typical digital camera to a PC. Label your diagram clearly.

Flow diagrams

Flow diagrams or flow charts are used to illustrate a sequence of events. They are often used to describe engineering processes such as those concerned with stages in the manufacture of a product or the maintenance of a piece of equipment (see Figure 3.19).

Schematic diagrams

Schematic diagrams are used to show how components are connected together in electrical, pneumatic and hydraulic circuits. Schematic diagrams use standard symbols and the links between them are shown with lines. There are several types of schematic diagram including those used for electrical and electronic circuits, pneumatic (compressed air) and hydraulic (compressed fluid) circuits.

Circuit diagrams

Circuit diagrams or circuit schematics are used to show how components are connected in an electric or electronic circuit. The components (such as resistors, capacitors, and diodes) are represented by symbols and the electrical connections between the components drawn using straight lines. It is worth remembering that the position of a component in a circuit diagram does not represent its actual position in the real circuit.

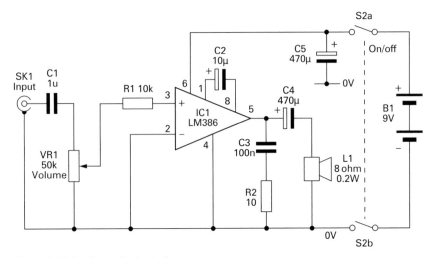

Figure 3.20 An electronic circuit diagram

Hands On

Take a careful look at the electronic circuit diagram shown in Figure 3.20 and use it to answer the following questions:

1. What type of device is IC1?
2. What is the supply voltage for the circuit?
3. What is the value of (a) R1 and (b) C2?
4. Which two pins on IC1 are taken to 0V?
5. What is the function of VR1?
6. Which is the signal output pin on IC1?

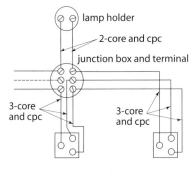

Figure 3.21 A wiring diagram

Wiring diagrams

A wiring diagram is another form of schematic diagram. It shows the physical connections between electrical and electronic components rather than the electrical connections between them.

Pneumatic and hydraulic circuits

Schematic diagrams are also used to represent **pneumatic** circuits and **hydraulic** circuits. Pneumatic circuits and hydraulic circuits share the same symbols. You can tell which circuit is which because pneumatic circuits should have open arrowheads, while hydraulic circuits should have solid arrowheads. Also, pneumatic circuits exhaust to the atmosphere, while hydraulic circuits have to have a return path to a fluid reservoir.

Key terms

Pneumatic – a system that uses compressed gas (usually air) to produce motion

Hydraulic – a system that uses compressed liquid (usually special hydraulic fluid based on oil) to produce motion

Figure 3.22 shows a simple hydraulic circuit where the components are represented by standard symbols just as the electronic components were drawn in symbolic form in the circuit schematic shown in Figure 3.20.

Just as electrical and electronic circuit diagrams may have corresponding layout and wiring diagrams, so do hydraulic, pneumatic and plumbing circuits. Only this time the wiring diagram becomes a piping diagram.

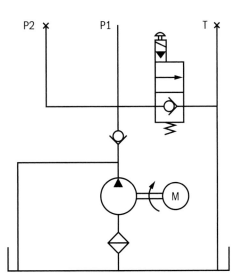

Figure 3.22 An example of a hydraulic circuit diagram

QUICK CHECK

What is the difference between a pneumatic circuit and a hydraulic circuit?

Quick Tip

It is well worth taking the time to learn a CAD package. If you do not have the opportunity to take a course you can always download a free evaluation version of the software. By just trying a few simple exercises you will find that you quickly get up to speed with it.

Hands On

Use a CAD package to create a detail drawing of a simple engineered part or component such as a flange or mounting bracket.

Using CAD

Computer-aided design (CAD) has now largely replaced manual methods used for producing formal engineering drawing. CAD software is used with a computer and the drawing produced on the computer screen is saved in a computer file on disk. Modern CAD packages are often linked into more complex computer-aided manufacturing (CAM) systems which allow drawing data to be passed on electronically to the software and machine tools used in the manufacturing process.

Modern networked CAD/CAM and computer-aided engineering systems (CAE) have made it possible to share data and drawings over a network and also make them available to computer numerically controlled (CNC) machine tools that carry out automated manufacturing operations.

Figure 3.23 shows a general arrangement (GA) drawing produced using a popular CAD program. Drawings like this show how a complex product is assembled from its component parts. Product design involves a great deal of 3D work in the initial stages of designing a product before any of the parts or components are manufactured.

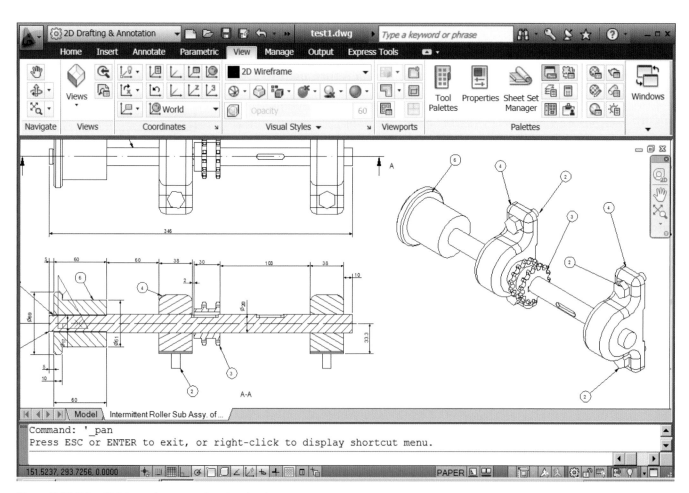

Figure 3.23 Using CAD to produce an engineering drawing

Assembly diagrams and exploded views

Assembly diagrams and exploded views show how a product is taken apart and reassembled. You can gain a very good idea of how something is put together by drawing the individual component parts separately but in approximately the same physical relationship as when assembled. Exploded views can be extremely useful when a product has to be serviced or maintained. A service or maintenance engineer has only to take a look at an exploded diagram to see how the various parts fit together. A typical assembly diagram for an electrical control box is shown in Figure 3.24.

Hands On

Obtain an assembly drawing for an engineered product with which you are familiar. Use the drawing to identify key components and the sequence in which they are assembled.

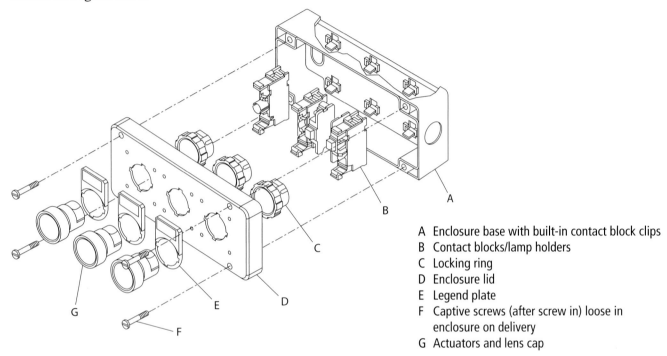

A   Enclosure base with built-in contact block clips
B   Contact blocks/lamp holders
C   Locking ring
D   Enclosure lid
E   Legend plate
F   Captive screws (after screw in) loose in enclosure on delivery
G   Actuators and lens cap

Figure 3.24 An assembly diagram for an electrical control box

QUICK CHECK

1   Explain the advantages of using a CAD system to create, store and distribute an engineering drawing.
2   Explain the purpose of an assembly diagram. What makes this type of diagram different from a general arrangement diagram?

Charts, graphs and tables

Numerical engineering data is often presented in the form of a graph, chart or table. This makes the information easy to use and it also provides us with a visual representation of a trend or tendency in the data. For example, the force applied by a pneumatic ram may increase in accordance with the square of the velocity of the ram. This relationship can be understood more easily if the data is presented in the form of a graph rather than as a long list of values in a table.

Charts and graphs

Charts and graphs provide a simple pictorial way of illustrating data. Typical examples are shown in Figures 3.25 and 3.26. Notice how easy it is to spot a trend when data is presented in this way.

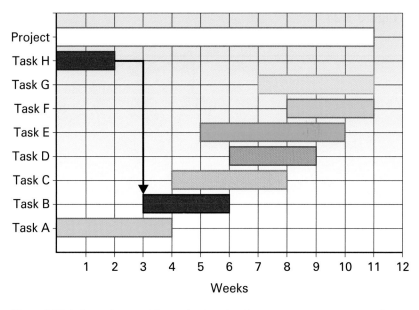

Figure 3.25 A Gantt chart used for production planning

Hands On

Use the Test Chart shown in Figure 3.26 to answer the following questions:

1. What was the average value of the observed data?

2. Were any of the observed values below the lower acceptance limit?

3. How many observed values were outside the acceptance limits shown on the chart?

4. Is there an overall trend in the data and, if so, in which direction is it?

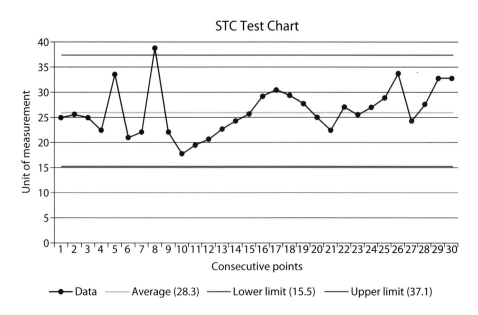

Figure 3.26 A test chart used for quality control

Tables

Numerical engineering data is frequently shown in the form of tables of data. Typical examples are those that show the dimensions of screw threads, limits and fits, welding data, tapping data, wire gauges and current capacities, etc. You will find several of these in use in the workshop and you should get into the habit of using them when the need arises.

Standard wire gauge (SWG)	Wire diameter or sheet thickness
SWG 10	3.25 mm
SWG 12	2.64 mm
SWG 14	2.03 mm
SWG 16	1.63 mm
SWG 18	1.22 mm
SWG 20	0.914 mm

Table 3.02 Standard wire gauge (SWG) data represented in a table

Hands On

The table above shows the wire diameter or sheet thickness that corresponds to different values of Standard Wire Gauge (SWG). Use the table to answer the following questions:

1. What do you notice about the SWG rating as the thickness or diameter increases?
2. What sheet thickness corresponds to 14 SWG?
3. What is the nearest standard wire gauge corresponding to a sheet thickness of 1.5 mm?
4. Will a wire of 14 SWG pass through a hole having a diameter of 2 mm? Explain your answer.
5. Use Internet or library resources to investigate the American Wire Gauge (AWG). How does this differ from the Standard Wire Gauge?

Sources of data

When creating a drawing or producing a document you may need to refer to various sources of data. The data needs to be:

- **relevant** – it needs to refer to the right part, component or material
- **valid** – it needs to come from an approved source (such as the original manufacturer or supplier)
- **precise** – it needs to be exact and not merely approximate
- **accurate** – it needs to be correct and stated to the required accuracy
- **comprehensive** – it needs to contain all of the required detail
- **current** – it needs to be up to date and must take into account any changes or modifications.

As an example, assume that you have been given the task of replacing the mains transformer fitted to an item of electrical equipment. You will need to refer to a variety of documentation in order to establish the suitability of a particular replacement part. You will need to know the power rating of the transformer (stated in VA), the primary and secondary voltages, the load current placed on each secondary winding, and the required regulation (i.e. the ability of the transformer to maintain its secondary voltage when placed on load).

Having established the electrical specifications for the transformer you will now need to investigate the physical dimensions of the replacement transformer and the means by which it is mounted. All of this information should be available from the manufacturer's data sheet but when there is any doubt you might need to obtain a sample of the part and make your own measurements to fill in the gaps in the data (for example, the space between fixing centres). Most manufacturers will be able to supply you with a detailed drawing of the component but if this is not the case you will need to obtain a sample and make these measurements yourself.

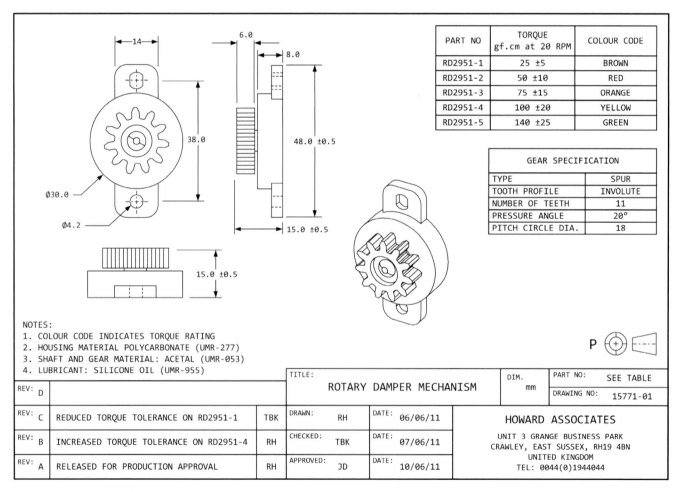

PART NO	TORQUE gf.cm at 20 RPM	COLOUR CODE
RD2951-1	25 ±5	BROWN
RD2951-2	50 ±10	RED
RD2951-3	75 ±15	ORANGE
RD2951-4	100 ±20	YELLOW
RD2951-5	140 ±25	GREEN

GEAR SPECIFICATION	
TYPE	SPUR
TOOTH PROFILE	INVOLUTE
NUMBER OF TEETH	11
PRESSURE ANGLE	20°
PITCH CIRCLE DIA.	18

NOTES:
1. COLOUR CODE INDICATES TORQUE RATING
2. HOUSING MATERIAL POLYCARBONATE (UMR-277)
3. SHAFT AND GEAR MATERIAL: ACETAL (UMR-053)
4. LUBRICANT: SILICONE OIL (UMR-955)

REV: D			TITLE: ROTARY DAMPER MECHANISM	DIM. mm	PART NO: SEE TABLE
REV: C	REDUCED TORQUE TOLERANCE ON RD2951-1	TBK	DRAWN: RH DATE: 06/06/11	DRAWING NO: 15771-01
REV: B	INCREASED TORQUE TOLERANCE ON RD2951-4	RH	CHECKED: TBK DATE: 07/06/11	HOWARD ASSOCIATES
REV: A	RELEASED FOR PRODUCTION APPROVAL	RH	APPROVED: JD DATE: 10/06/11	UNIT 3 GRANGE BUSINESS PARK CRAWLEY, EAST SUSSEX, RH19 4BN UNITED KINGDOM TEL: 0044(0)1944044

Figure 3.27 An example of comprehensive information provided by a part supplier and conveyed by a single drawing sheet

Hands On

The rotary damper mechanism shown in Figure 3.27 provides resistance and slows the movement of applications in which devices open and close such as access panels, doors, covers and trays. The mechanism uses the principle of fluid resistance to dampen movement. Look carefully at the drawing and use it to answer the following questions:

1. When was the drawing produced?

2. Has the drawing been approved and how do you know?

3. What type of gear is used in the mechanism?

4. What revisions have been made to the drawing?

QUICK CHECK

1 What are the advantages of using charts, graphs and tables to show engineering information?

2 Give an example of the use of **(a)** charts and **(b)** graphs in engineering.

3 List five important considerations when selecting a source of engineering data.

Care and control of documents and drawings

It is important to ensure that drawings and documents are stored and used correctly. This will ensure that they are not damaged as a result of physical handling or the environment in which they are used. Documents should be stored in appropriate cabinets well away from dust, dirt, oil and grease. Some means for controlling the issue (and return!) of documents is also an important requirement, particularly where a number of people need to have access to a document. Many companies have a technical library and a person appointed to be responsible for it. This operates in a similar way to that of a public library, where books and other materials are available for loan to borrowers.

Like the formal drawings that we introduced earlier, engineering documents should be clearly marked with the originator's name, the issue number and/or the date of issue, and the date of any subsequent revisions or modifications. Many companies are now moving to the electronic storage of drawings and documents. This has the obvious advantage that the original drawings or documents are stored in a form that is very secure and also that they can be updated very easily whenever the need arises.

Document control is an important aspect of the operation of all large engineering companies and the use of computerised systems has made this much easier and more effective. Damaged or lost drawings should always be reported to your supervisor or another responsible person.

Key term

Controlled document – a controlled document is a reference document which, through the course of its lifecycle may be reviewed, modified and re-issued several times

Controlled documents

Many engineering documents are referred to as **controlled documents**. The term can apply to a wide variety of engineering information including drawings, specifications, procedures, data sheets, contracts, application notes and plans. If a controlled document is changed, a record of the change has to be made and, equally important, employees must get into the habit of checking to see if documentation they are using is the current version.

Hands On

1. Describe the procedures for:
    (a) reporting discrepancies in data or documents
    (b) reporting lost or damaged documents within your company.

2. Describe the care and control procedures for documents in your company including:
    (a) reporting errors and discrepancies
    (b) dealing with damaged or lost documents.

If a controlled document is changed everyone who might need to use it must (a) know that a change has been made and (b) have access to the current version of the document. This means that versions of a document and any revisions made to it need to be clearly identified. This is more easily achieved with electronic document storage than with printed documents simply because there is only one definitive source of each document rather than multiple paper copies which can easily become outdated because they are held in various places.

Hands On

Obtain an example of a controlled document and use it to answer the following questions:

1. What is the title and purpose of the document?
2. What is the name of the person who authorised the document?
3. What is the date of the document?
4. Have any changes been made to the document and how do you know?

QUICK CHECK

What is a controlled document and why does it need to be controlled?

Lucy Ackland is a Design Development Technician. She works for a leading UK-based company involved with the development of highly accurate measuring equipment. Lucy decided to take a career in engineering and has been with the company for six years since leaving school.

Lucy started her employment as an apprentice straight after taking her GCSEs. Then she completed a year of off-the-job training and returned to the company, continuing her training by attending college for one day each week. At the end of her apprenticeship she was offered a permanent job in the company.

Lucy works as a member of a small team, seeing design and development projects through to the end before they enter the market. Her work involves testing that a product will work correctly and conform to the original design requirements and specification. Any faults that she finds will usually require further investigation before a particular part is ready to go into production.

Communicating information is a large part of Lucy's everyday work. She has to read and understand drawings, specifications and a wide variety of supporting documentation – just like the examples that you have met in this chapter. Lucy needs to work with other engineers but first she needs to make sure that *she* understands the problems so that she can pass on all of the relevant information to everyone else who needs to know.

CHECK YOUR KNOWLEDGE

1 Whenever the dimension of a part is changed:

   a a technical report should be issued

   b a new application note should be written

   c no changes to documentation are necessary

   d relevant diagrams and drawings should be revised and updated

2 The reference numbers for the individual components used in a mechanical assembly will be found in:

   a a parts list

   b a specification

   c a technical report

   d an application note

3 Which one of the following appears in the title block of a drawing?

   a A list of materials

   b The dimensions of each component

   c The company name and contact information

   d Isometric or orthographic views, as appropriate

4 Which one of the following is a type of schematic drawing?

   a A bar chart

   b A circuit diagram

   c An isometric view

   d A general arrangement (GA) diagram

5 Changes made to update a drawing are found in the:

   a parts list

   b revision list

   c isometric view

   d supporting documentation

6 A controlled document must always:

   a remain unchanged and unmodified

   b be clearly marked as such and stored in a secure place

   c be revised whenever the need arises and earlier versions withdrawn

   d be copied and circulated widely in both paper and electronic versions

7 Document control is easier to implement when documents and drawings are stored:

   a as hard-copy printouts in desk drawers

   b in electronic form on a network server

   c on compact disks and circulated by post

   d on a number of local computers and circulated as email attachments.

8 The sequence of events that take place in an engineering process are best described using:

   a a block diagram

   b an auxiliary diagram

   c a flow chart

   d a general arrangement diagram

9 A trend in data can best be viewed using:

   a a table

   b a data sheet

   c a flow chart

   d a line graph

10 When dismantling a complex engineered product such as a motor or gearbox it is important to have:

   a a detail drawing

   b an isometric drawing

   c an exploded view

   d a formal drawing

Index